PASSION PLAY
Oberammergau 2022

PASSION PLAY

Oberammergau 2022

Published by the
Municipality of Oberammergau

Theater der Zeit

Christian Stückl

Director

Stefan Hageneier

Set and costume designer

Markus Zwink

Musical director and composer

Eva Kammerer

Dr. Christian Wolf

Conductors

Abdullah Kenan Karaca

Deputy director

Birgit Guðjónsdóttir

Photographer

CONTENT

FOREWORD

Almost 400 years ago Oberammergau was seized by the turmoil of the Thirty Years' War. Soldiers rampaged throughout the land, famine followed and the Black Death held the people in its clutches. According to an old legend, a man named Kaspar Schisler brought the plague to the village in 1632 and within just a few days of his arrival around eighty adult residents were dead. The records are patchy and do not include children in the tally, so the mortality rate was probably much higher. In the hour of their distress, the people of Oberammergau came together and vowed to perform the play "of the suffering, death and resurrection of our Lord Jesus Christ" every ten years from that point. At the time, the play was staged by the Catholic Church, which had several large monasteries – Ettal, Rottenbuch, Steingaden and Polling – in a region which was firmly in its grasp. It moulded the thinking of the inhabitants, many of whom were poor peasants who worked as bonded labourers with few rights. Fear reigned: preachers presented God as an angry old man who punished people for their sins. No one knew about viruses or bacteria at the time, so this cruel disease, which was responsible for the death of thousands, young and old, could only be interpreted as God's wrath. Many sought remedy in focusing on the sufferings – the "Passion" – of Christ, who died "for the sins of humanity". A huge number of Passion Plays emerged across Bavaria. Over 400 locations performed the story of the Passion in this era and, legend has it, cast out the plague so successfully that it ceased its deadly work.

When the corona epidemic forced us to cancel the Passion Play in spring 2020, there were frequent references to the old Oberammergau plague story. Several people asked me if we were thinking about taking a new vow. I had to laugh: those of us who believe in God have long shared a completely different image of the deity. Today, none of us imagines an angry old man with a white beard sitting on his throne up in Heaven, dreaming up diseases, wars and famines as punishment for "sinful mankind" which refuses to submit to his will. Today, we know that it is we who are responsible for the suffering and misery in our world. It is not God who thinks up wars, we do. God is not at fault for the hunger in the world, we are. Our image of God and the world has changed fundamentally.

And yet we hold on to this ancient tradition. Every ten years we perform the story of a man who travelled through the desert of Galilee more than 2,000 years ago, stirred up the cities of Capernaum and Jerusalem and was crucified at the age of 33. In many other sites, Passion Plays disappeared without a trace long ago. But not in Oberammergau. Here it is a living tradition, maintained with an enthusiasm which transcends the generations. Sometimes it seems like a miracle: a village transforms into a theatre, thousands of spectators come from all over the world and marvel at hundreds of long-haired and bearded amateur actors, singers and musicians, who come together on stage and fervently perform the life of Jesus. How does it happen? How do you get almost an entire village to come together and act out a story that is undeniably old, for some even outdated and antiquated? I believe the only way is to keep re-examining the story. No lack of questions arise in the process. The performance tradition dates back almost 400 years and along the way it has accrued rules that are no longer viable today. Until the 1990s performers had to belong to one of the two major churches, Catholic or Protestant. But Oberammergau changed long ago and residents who have left the church are now welcome to perform, so too our Muslim villagers. Women have the same rights as men – something that seems self-evident now yet was anything but prior to 1990. And in the future we will need to keep working on integrating people into the play rather than shutting them out.

Another point we address is the impact of the play throughout its history. Profound anti-Jewish sentiment was already apparent in early Christian Europe, its central tenet the accusation that Jews were to blame for the death of Christ. This attitude was reflected in the Passion Play. It completely ignored the fact that it was the Roman Pontius Pilate who condemned Christ to death and that the key figures in Christian belief – Jesus, Mary, Mary Magdalene, Peter and John – were observant Jews who at no time considered establishing a new church. The Passion Play tells the story of a young man who even as a child, as the Gospel of Luke tells us, had a great passion for the Torah, the holy scripture of the Jews, and who argued vehemently about its interpretation with scholars. We have long been aware that Jesus was a mighty warrior for his God – the God of Abraham, Isaac and Jacob – and yet he and his name

have been misused to ostracise, persecute, imprison and murder Jews. Let there be no doubt: in Oberammergau, in the play, anti-Semitism has no place, and it has no place in the lives of the performers either.

No less important is the question of Jesus himself, his disciples and all the other characters who populate the play. What kind of person was he, what drove him and those around him? Early on he left his childhood home, his mother and his siblings. He was thrown out of the synagogue in Nazareth when his interpretation of the Torah met with resistance. "A prophet is not without honour, but in his own country, and among his own kin, and in his own house" – this formulation of Jesus remains common to this day. In the ensuing years he most likely wandered the cities of Tiberias and Capernaum, looking out for the socially marginalised – prostitutes, widows and their children. Jesus was already 30 years old when he experienced his religious awakening in the desert. People flocked to him by the Sea of Galilee, left their jobs and their families behind to follow him. The rich were anathema to Jesus. His desire was for unconditional peace and he told his followers that they should love their enemies. "Whosoever shall smite thee on thy right cheek, turn to him the other also!" It is a verse we are unable to bear, an attitude we believe doesn't work – not in our own lives and certainly not in the world. And today we see the consequences in Ukraine, in Syria, in Yemen, in Afghanistan and in many other places in the world.

Christian Stückl

Page 6/7: Choristers and actors commemorate the vow of 1633

9

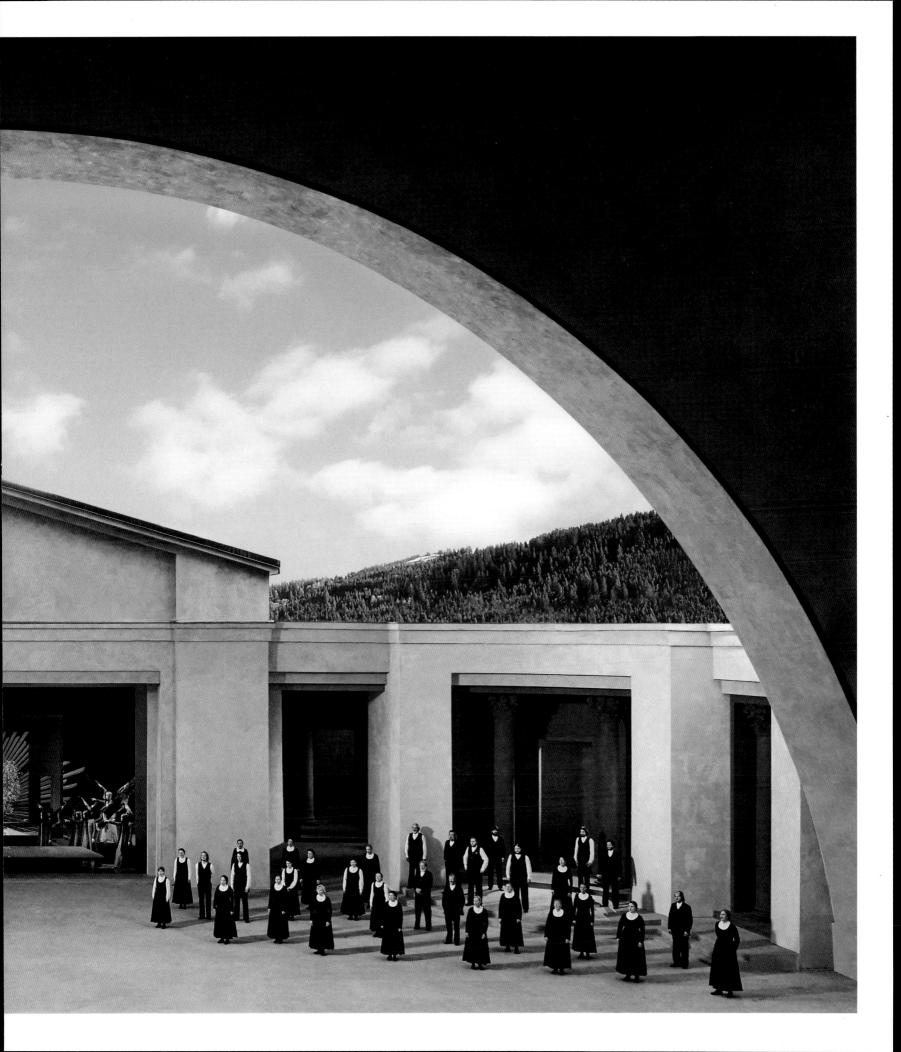

The Expulsion from the Garden of Eden

So God created man in his own image, in the image of God created he him; male and female created he them. And the LORD God took the man, and put him into the garden of Eden to dress it and to keep it. And the LORD God commanded the man, saying, Of every tree of the garden thou mayest freely eat: But of the tree of the knowledge of good and evil, thou shalt not eat of it. Now the serpent was more subtil than any beast of the field. And he said: For God doth know that in the day ye eat thereof, then your eyes shall be opened, and ye shall be as gods, knowing good and evil. They took of the fruit thereof, and did eat. And the eyes of them both were opened, and they knew that they were naked. And the LORD God called unto Adam, and said unto him, Where art thou? And he said, I heard thy voice in the garden, and I was afraid, because I was naked; and I hid myself. And the LORD God said, Who told thee that thou wast naked? Hast thou eaten of the tree, whereof I commanded thee that thou shouldest not eat? And the LORD God said, Behold, the man is become as one of us, to know good and evil: and now, lest he put forth his hand, and take also of the tree of life, and eat, and live for ever: Therefore the LORD God sent him forth from the garden of Eden, to till the ground from whence he was taken. So he drove out the man; and he placed at the east of the garden of Eden Cherubims, and a flaming sword which turned every way, to keep the way of the tree of life.

Genesis 1,27; Genesis 2,15 ff.; Genesis 3,1 ff.

JESUS ENTERS JERUSALEM

And the Jews' passover was at hand, and Jesus went up to Jerusalem. When they drew nigh unto Jerusalem, and were come to Bethphage, unto the mount of Olives, then sent Jesus two disciples, Saying unto them, Go into the village over against you, and straightway ye shall find an ass tied, and a colt with her: loose them, and bring them unto me. And the disciples went, and did as Jesus commanded them, And brought the ass, and the colt, and put on them their clothes, and they set him thereon. All this was done, that it might be fulfilled which was spoken by the prophet, saying, Tell ye the daughter of Sion, Behold, thy King cometh unto thee, meek, and sitting upon an ass, and a colt the foal of an ass.

And there followed him great multitudes of people from Galilee, and from Decapolis, and from Jerusalem, and from Judaea, and from beyond Jordan. And a very great multitude spread their garments in the way; others cut down branches from the trees, and strawed them in the way. And the multitudes that went before, and that followed, cried, saying, Hosanna to the Son of David: Blessed is he that cometh in the name of the Lord; Hosanna in the highest. And when he was come into Jerusalem, all the city was moved, saying, Who is this? And the multitude said, This is Jesus the prophet of Nazareth of Galilee.

And he lifted up his eyes and said, Blessed be ye poor: for yours is the kingdom of God. Blessed are ye that hunger now: for ye shall be filled. Blessed are ye that weep now: for ye shall laugh. But woe unto you that are rich! for ye have received your consolation. Woe unto you that are full! for ye shall hunger. Woe unto you that laugh now! for ye shall mourn and weep.
Matthew 21,1 ff.; Matthew 4,25; Luke 6,20 ff.

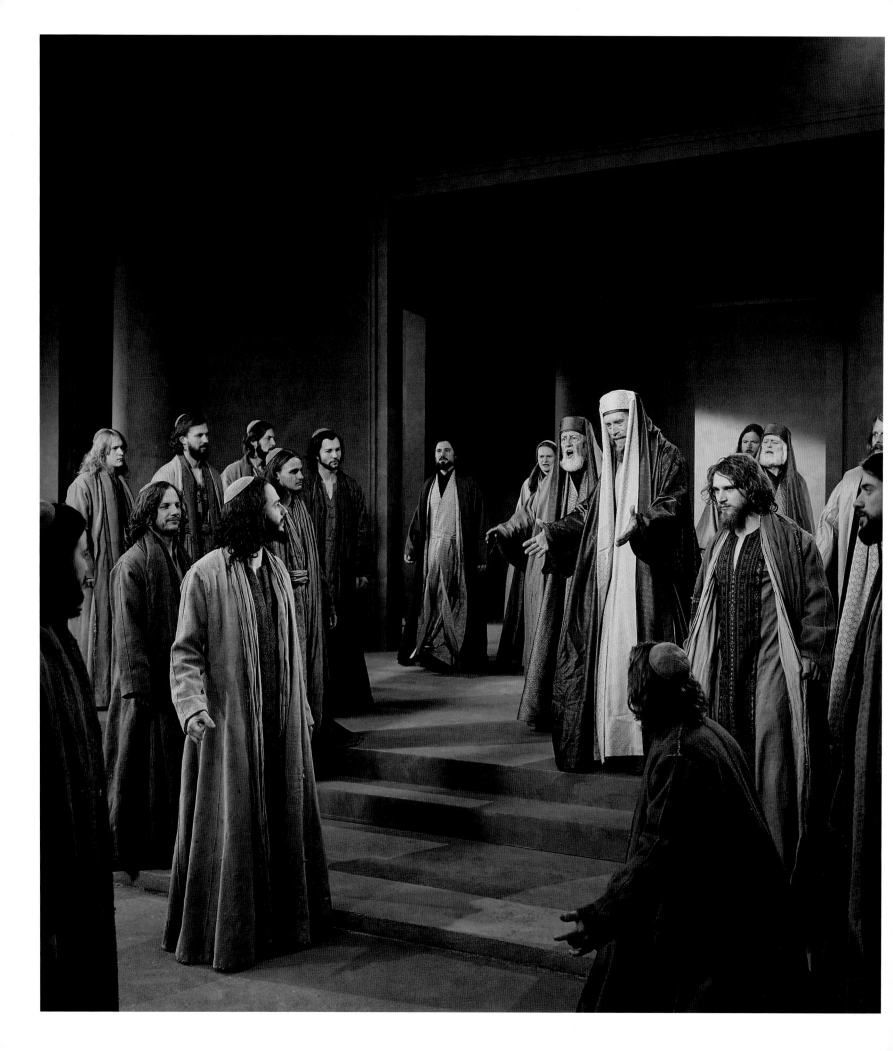

The Humiliation of the Israelites

Now these are the names of the children of Israel, which came into Egypt; every man and his household came with Jacob. Reuben, Simeon, Levi, and Judah, Issachar, Zebulun, and Benjamin, Dan, and Naphtali, Gad, and Asher. And all the souls that came out of the loins of Jacob were seventy souls. And the children of Israel were fruitful, and increased abundantly, and multiplied, and waxed exceeding mighty; and the land was filled with them. Now there arose up a new king over Egypt, which knew not Joseph. And he said unto his people, Behold, the people of the children of Israel are more and mightier than we: Come on, let us deal wisely with them; lest they multiply, and it come to pass, that, when there falleth out any war, they join also unto our enemies, and fight against us, and so get them up out of the land. Therefore they did set over them taskmasters to afflict them with their burdens. And they built for Pharaoh treasure cities, Pithom and Raamses. But the more they afflicted them, the more they multiplied and grew. And the Egyptians made the children of Israel to serve with rigour: And they made their lives bitter with hard bondage, in morter, and in brick, and in all manner of service in the field: all their service, wherein they made them serve, was with rigour. And Pharaoh charged all his people, saying, Every son that is born ye shall cast into the river.

Exodus 1 ff.

JESUS IN BETHANY

And he left them, and went out of the city into Bethany; and he lodged there.

And he said unto his disciples: Ye have heard that it hath been said, Thou shalt love thy neighbour, and hate thine enemy. But I say unto you, Love your enemies, bless them that curse you, do good to them that hate you, and pray for them which despitefully use you, and persecute you; That ye may be the children of your Father which is in heaven: for he maketh his sun to rise on the evil and on the good, and sendeth rain on the just and on the unjust. For if ye love them which love you, what reward have ye? do not even the publicans the same? And if ye salute your brethren only, what do ye more than others? do not even the publicans so? Be ye therefore perfect, even as your Father which is in heaven is perfect. And these twelve Jesus sent forth, and commanded them, saying, go to the lost sheep of the house of Israel. And as ye go, preach, saying, The kingdom of heaven is at hand. Heal the sick, cleanse the lepers, raise the dead, cast out devils: freely ye have received, freely give.

Behold, I send you forth as sheep in the midst of wolves: be ye therefore wise as serpents, and harmless as doves. But beware of men: for they will deliver you up to the councils, and they will scourge you in their synagogues; And the brother shall deliver up the brother to death, and the father the child: and the children shall rise up against their parents, and cause them to be put to death. And ye shall be hated of all men for my name's sake: but he that endureth to the end shall be saved.

There was a man of the Pharisees, named Nicodemus, a ruler of the Jews: The same came to Jesus, and said unto him, Rabbi, we know that thou art a teacher come from God: for no man can do these miracles that thou doest, except God be with him.

Now when Jesus was in Bethany, in the house of Simon the leper, There came unto him a woman having an alabaster box of very precious ointment, and poured it on his head, as he sat at meat. But when his disciples saw it, they had indignation, saying, To what purpose is this waste? For this ointment might have been sold for much, and given to the poor. When Jesus understood it, he said unto them, Why trouble ye the woman? for she hath wrought a good work upon me.

Matthew 21,17; Matthew 5,43 ff.; Matthew 10,5 ff.; Matthew 26,6 ff.; John 3,1 ff.

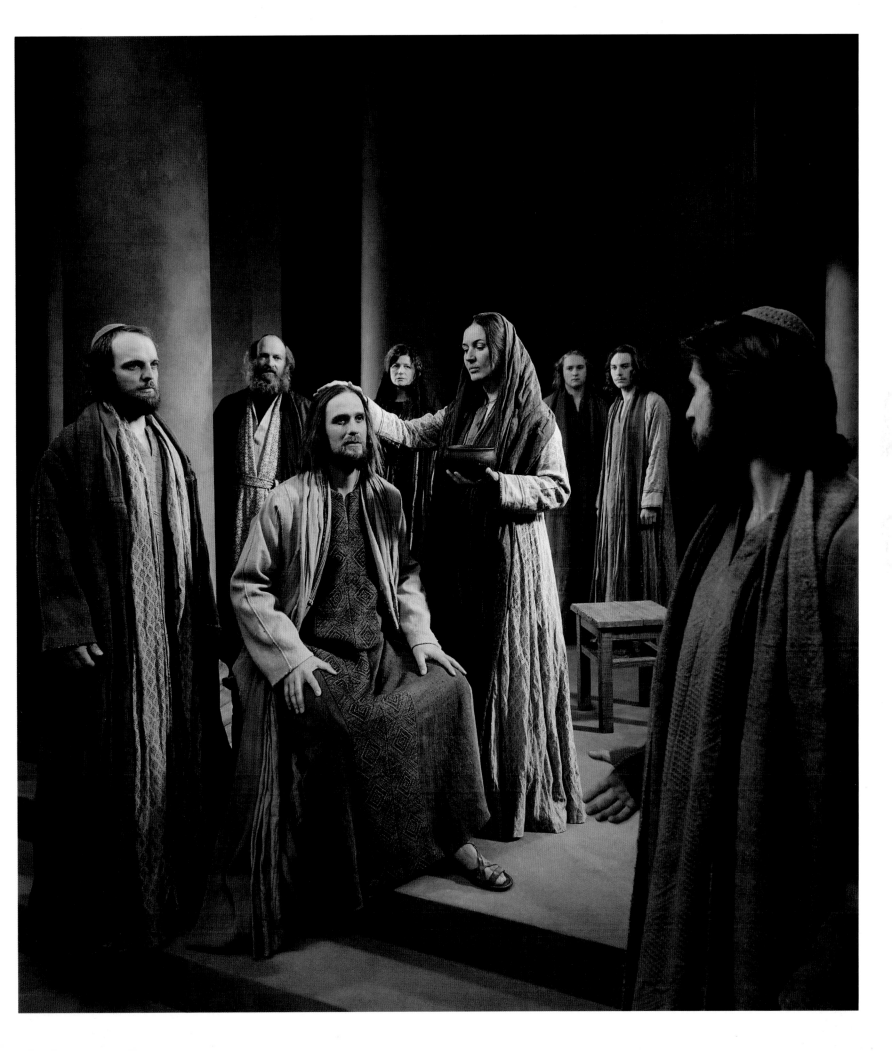

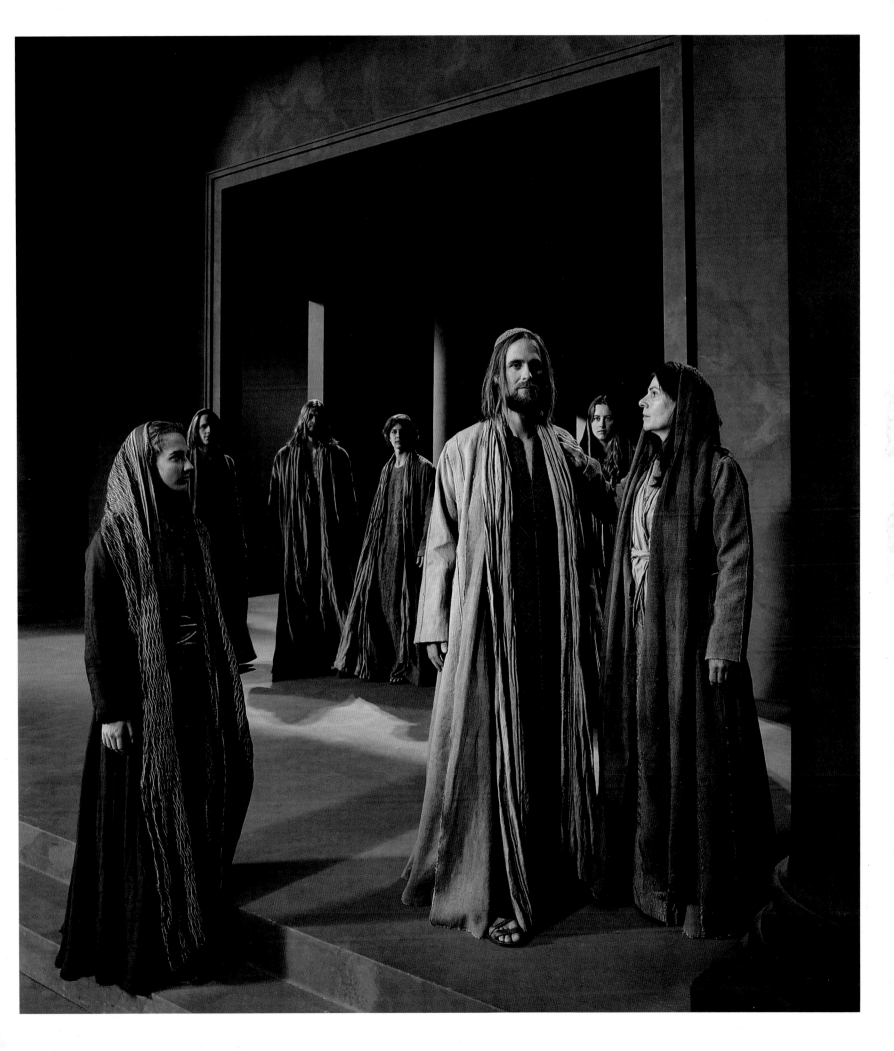

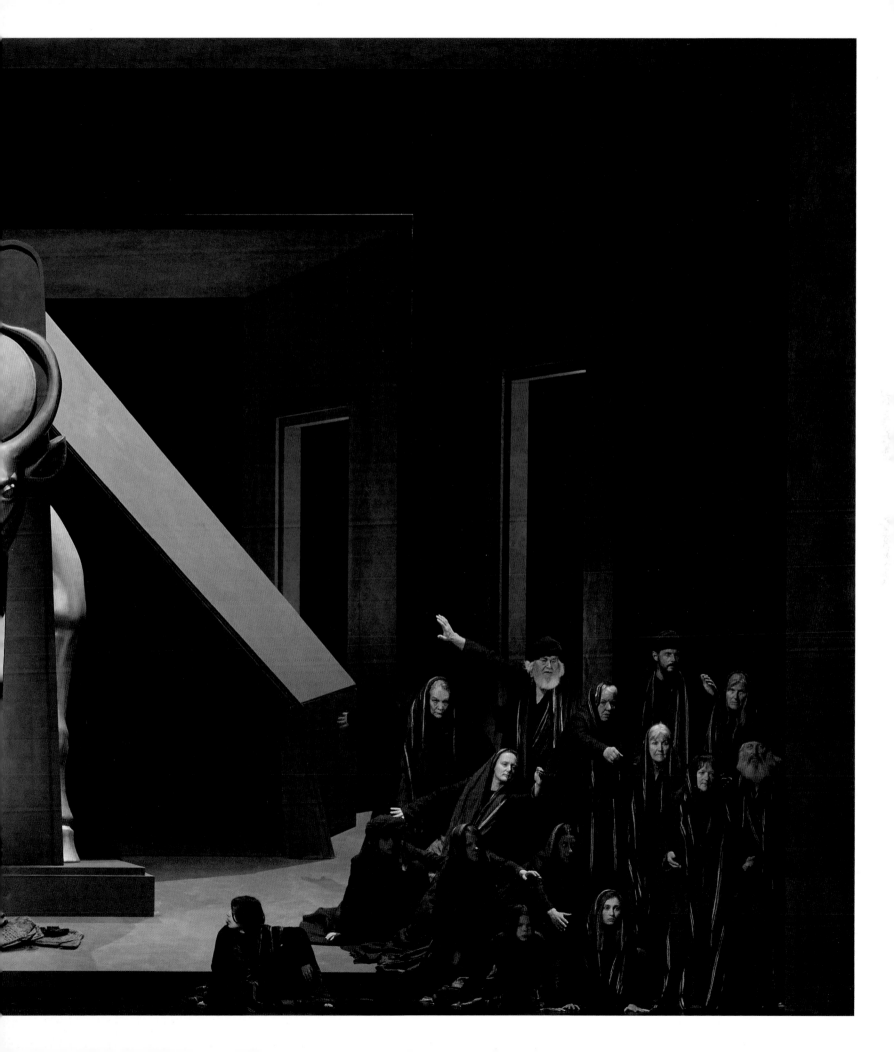

The Golden Calf

In the third month, when the children of Israel were gone forth out of the land of Egypt, the same day came they into the wilderness of Sinai. And Moses went up unto God.

And when the people saw that Moses delayed to come down out of the mount, the people gathered themselves together unto Aaron, and said unto him, Up, make us gods, which shall go before us; for as for this Moses, the man that brought us up out of the land of Egypt, we wot not what is become of him. And Aaron said unto them, Break off the golden earrings, which are in the ears of your wives, of your sons, and of your daughters, and bring them unto me. And all the people brake off the golden earrings which were in their ears, and brought them unto Aaron. And he received them at their hand, and fashioned it with a graving tool, after he had made it a molten calf: and they said, These be thy gods, O Israel, which brought thee up out of the land of Egypt. And they rose up early on the morrow, and offered burnt offerings, and brought peace offerings; and the people sat down to eat and to drink, and rose up to play.

And it came to pass, as soon as Moses came nigh unto the camp, that he saw the calf, and the dancing: and Moses' anger waxed hot, and he cast the tables out of his hands, and brake them beneath the mount. And he took the calf which they had made, and burnt it in the fire.

Exodus 19,1 ff.; Exodus 32,1 ff.

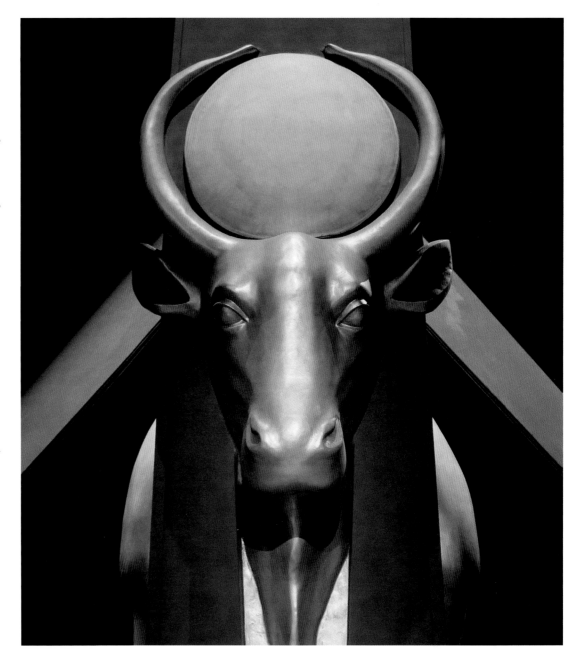

THE CLEANSING OF THE TEMPLE

And they come to Jerusalem: and Jesus went into the temple, and began to cast out them that sold and bought in the temple, and overthrew the tables of the moneychangers, and the seats of them that sold doves; And would not suffer that any man should carry any vessel through the temple. And he taught, saying unto them, Is it not written, My house shall be called of all nations the house of prayer? but ye have made it a den of thieves.

Then spake Jesus to the multitude, and to his disciples, Saying, The scribes and the Pharisees sit in Moses' seat: All therefore whatsoever they bid you observe, that observe and do; but do not ye after their works: for they say, and do not. For they bind heavy burdens and grievous to be borne, and lay them on men's shoulders; but they themselves will not move them with one of their fingers. But all their works they do for to be seen of men: they make broad their phylacteries, and enlarge the borders of their garments. But woe unto you, scribes and Pharisees, hypocrites! for ye shut up the kingdom of heaven against men: for ye neither go in yourselves, neither suffer ye them that are entering to go in. Woe unto you, scribes and Pharisees, hypocrites! for ye devour widows' houses, and for a pretence make long prayer: therefore ye shall receive the greater damnation. Woe unto you, scribes and Pharisees, hypocrites! for ye compass sea and land to make one proselyte, and when he is made, ye make him twofold more the child of hell than yourselves. Woe unto you, scribes and Pharisees, hypocrites! for ye pay tithe of mint and anise and cummin, and have omitted the weightier matters of the law, judgment, mercy, and faith: these ought ye to have done, and not to leave the other undone.

And one of the scribes came, and having heard them reasoning together, and perceiving that he had answered them well, asked him, Which is the first commandment of all? And Jesus answered him, The first of all the commandments is, Hear, O Israel; The Lord our God is one Lord: And thou shalt love the Lord thy God with all thy heart, and with all thy soul, and with all thy mind, and with all thy strength: this is the first commandment. And the second is like, namely this, Thou shalt love thy neighbour as thyself. There is none other commandment greater than these. *Mark 11,15 ff.; Matthew 23,1 ff.; Mark 12,28 ff.*

Israel and the Red Sea Crossing

And it was told the king of Egypt that the people fled: and the heart of Pharaoh was turned against the people. And he made ready his chariot, and took his people with him: And he took six hundred chosen chariots, and all the chariots of Egypt, and captains over every one of them. And he made ready his chariot, and took his people with him: And he took six hundred chosen chariots, and all the chariots of Egypt, and captains over every one of them.

And they were sore afraid: and the children of Israel cried out unto the LORD. And the LORD said unto Moses, speak unto the children of Israel, that they go forward: But lift thou up thy rod, and stretch out thine hand over the sea, and divide it: and the children of Israel shall go on dry ground through the midst of the sea. And I, behold, I will harden the hearts of the Egyptians, and they shall follow them: and I will get me honour upon Pharaoh, and upon all his host, upon his chariots, and upon his horsemen. And Moses stretched out his hand over the sea; and the LORD caused the sea to go back by a strong east wind all that night, and made the sea dry land, and the waters were divided. And the children of Israel went into the midst of the sea upon the dry ground: and the waters were a wall unto them on their right hand, and on their left. And the Egyptians pursued, and went in after them to the midst of the sea, even all Pharaoh's horses, his chariots, and his horsemen. And Moses stretched forth his hand over the sea, and the sea returned to his strength when the morning appeared; and the Egyptians fled against it; and the LORD overthrew the Egyptians in the midst of the sea.
Exodus 14,5 ff.

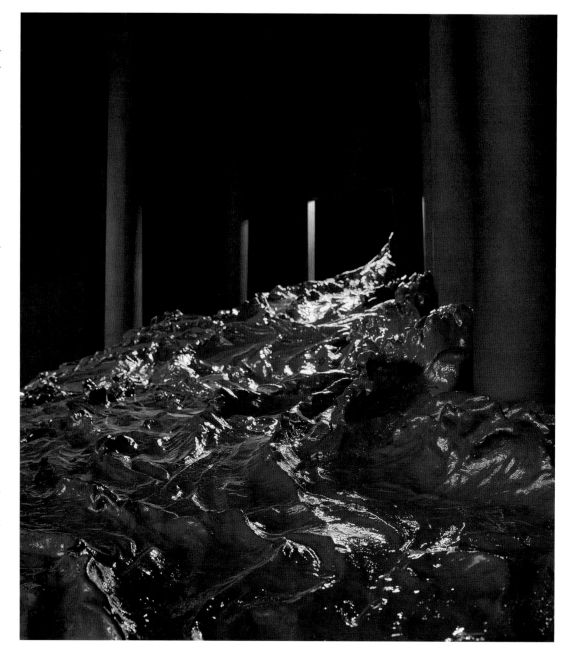

THE PRIESTS AND THE SCRIBES

Many of the people therefore, when they heard his saying, said, Of a truth this is the Prophet. Others said, This is the Messiah. So there was a division among the people because of him. And some of them would have taken him; but no man laid hands on him. Then came the officers to the chief priests and Pharisees; and they said unto them, Why have ye not brought him? The officers answered, Never man spake like this man. Then answered them the Pharisees, Are ye also deceived? Have any of the rulers or of the Pharisees believed on him? But this people who knoweth not the law are cursed. Nicodemus saith unto them, (he that came to Jesus by night, being one of them,) Doth our law judge any man, before it hear him, and know what he doeth? They answered and said unto him, Art thou also of Galilee? Search, and look: for out of Galilee ariseth no prophet.

But some of them went their ways to the Pharisees, and told them what things Jesus had done. Then gathered the chief priests and the Pharisees a council, and said, What do we? for this man doeth many miracles. If we let him thus alone, all men will believe on him: and the Romans shall come and take away both our place and nation. And one of them, named Caiaphas, being the high priest that same year, said unto them, Ye know nothing at all, Nor consider that it is expedient for us, that one man should die for the people, and that the whole nation perish not.

Then sought they for Jesus, and spake among themselves, as they stood in the temple, What think ye, that he will not come to the feast? Now both the chief priests and the Pharisees had given a commandment, that, if any man knew where he were, he should shew it, that they might take him.

John 7,40 ff.; John 11,46 ff.

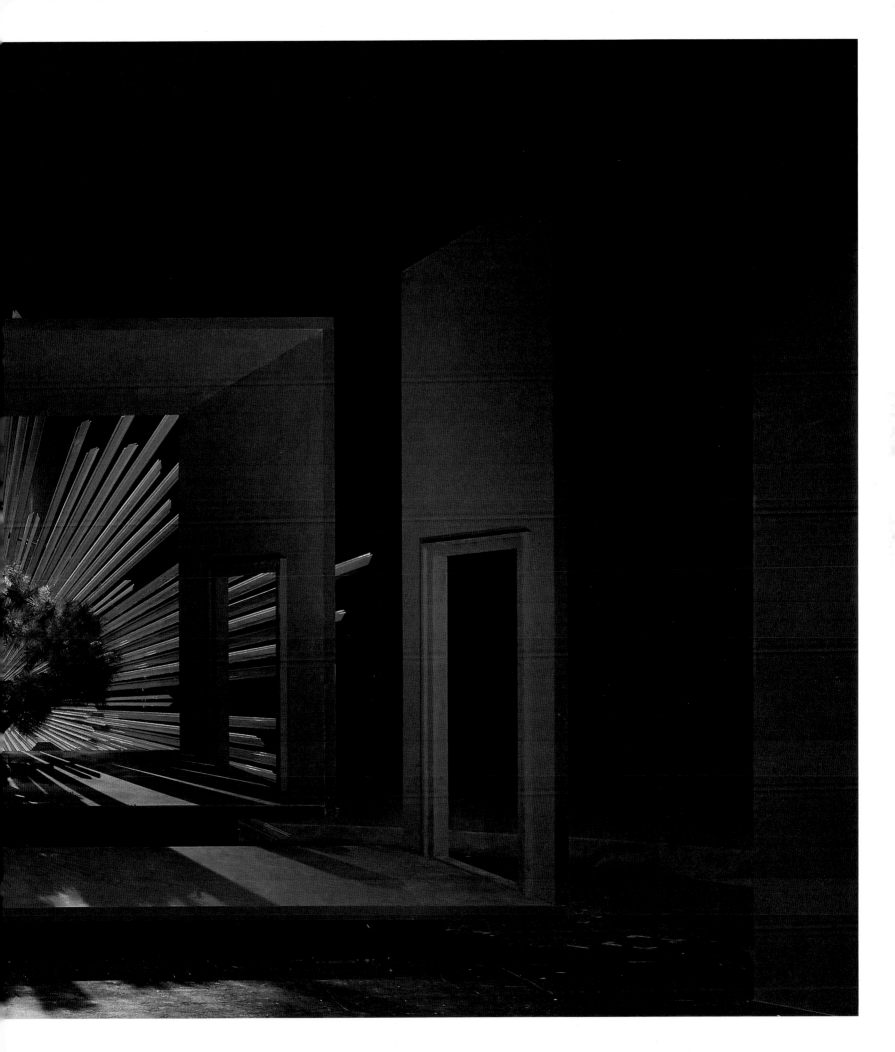

The Call of Moses

Moses kept the flock of Jethro his father in law, the priest of Midian: and he led the flock to the backside of the desert, and came to the mountain of God, even to Horeb. And the angel of the LORD appeared unto him in a flame of fire out of the midst of a bush. And Moses said, I will now turn aside, and see this great sight, why the bush is not burnt. And when the LORD saw that he turned aside to see, God called unto him out of the midst of the bush, and said, Moses, Moses. And he said, Here am I. And he said, Draw not nigh hither: put off thy shoes from off thy feet, for the place whereon thou standest is holy ground. Moreover he said, I am the God of thy father, the God of Abraham, the God of Isaac, and the God of Jacob. And Moses hid his face; for he was afraid to look upon God. And the LORD said, I have surely seen the affliction of my people which are in Egypt, and have heard their cry by reason of their taskmasters; for I know their sorrows; And I am come down to deliver them out of the hand of the Egyptians, and to bring them up out of that land unto a good land and a large, unto a land flowing with milk and honey; Now therefore, behold, the cry of the children of Israel is come unto me: and I have also seen the oppression wherewith the Egyptians oppress them. Come now therefore, and I will send thee unto Pharaoh, that thou mayest bring forth my people the children of Israel out of Egypt. And Moses said unto God, Who am I, that I should go unto Pharaoh, and that I should bring forth the children of Israel out of Egypt? And he said, Certainly I will be with thee; and this shall be a token unto thee, that I have sent thee: When thou hast brought forth the people out of Egypt, ye shall serve God upon this mountain.
Exodus 3,1 ff.

THE LAST SUPPER
AND THE ARREST OF JESUS

The first day of the feast of unleavened bread the disciples did as Jesus had appointed them; and they made ready the passover. Now when the even was come, he sat down with the twelve. And as they were eating, Jesus took bread, and blessed it, and brake it, and gave it to the disciples, and said, Take, eat; this is my body. And he took the cup, and gave thanks, and gave it to them, saying, Drink ye all of it; And when they had sung an hymn, they went out into the mount of Olives.

Then saith Jesus unto them, All ye shall be offended because of me this night. Peter answered and said unto him, Though all men shall be offended because of thee, yet will I never be offended. Jesus said unto him, Verily I say unto thee, That this night, before the cock crow, thou shalt deny me thrice. Peter said unto him, Though I should die with thee, yet will I not deny thee. Likewise also said all the disciples.

Then cometh Jesus with them unto a place called Gethsemane, and saith unto the disciples, Sit ye here, while I go and pray yonder. And he took with him Peter and the two sons of Zebedee, and began to be sorrowful and very heavy. Then saith he unto them, My soul is exceeding sorrowful, even unto death: tarry ye here, and watch with me. And he went a little farther, and fell on his face, and prayed, saying, O my Father, if it be possible, let this cup pass from me: nevertheless not as I will, but as thou wilt. And he cometh unto the disciples, and findeth them asleep, and saith unto Peter, What, could ye not watch with me one hour? Watch and pray, that ye enter not into temptation: the spirit indeed is willing, but the flesh is weak. Behold, the hour is at hand, and the Son of man is betrayed into the hands of sinners. Rise, let us be going: behold, he is at hand that doth betray me.

And while he yet spake, lo, Judas, one of the twelve, came, and with him a great multitude with swords and staves, from the chief priests and elders of the people. In that same hour said Jesus to the multitudes, Are ye come out as against a thief with swords and staves for to take me? I sat daily with you teaching in the temple, and ye laid no hold on me.
Matthew 26,17 ff.

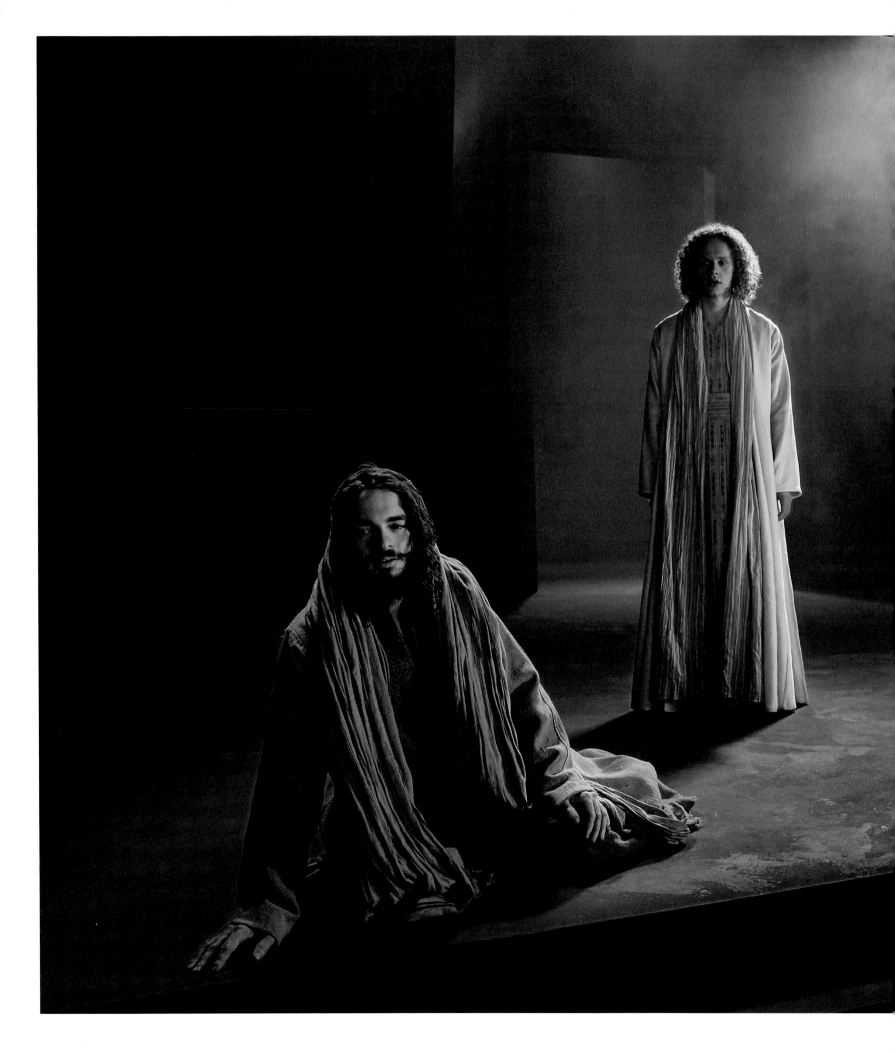

The Prophet Daniel in the Lions' Den

It pleased Darius to set over the kingdom princes, which should be over the whole kingdom; And over these three presidents; of whom Daniel was first. Then this Daniel was preferred above the presidents and princes, because an excellent spirit was in him; and the king thought to set him over the whole realm. Then the presidents and princes sought to find occasion against Daniel concerning the kingdom; Then said these men, We shall not find any occasion against this Daniel, except we find it against him concerning the law of his God.

Then these presidents and princes assembled together to the king, and said thus unto him, King Darius, live for ever. All the presidents of the kingdom have consulted together to establish a royal statute, and to make a firm decree, that whosoever shall ask a petition of any God or man for thirty days, save of thee, O king, he shall be cast into the den of lions. Wherefore king Darius signed the writing and the decree.

Now when Daniel knew that the writing was signed, he went into his house; he kneeled upon his knees three times a day, and prayed, and gave thanks before his God, as he did aforetime. Then these men assembled, and found Daniel praying and making supplication before his God. Then they came near, and spake before the king concerning the king's decree. They brought Daniel, and cast him into the den of lions.

Daniel 6,2 ff.

JESUS BEFORE THE HIGH COUNCIL

Then the band and the captain bound Jesus, And led him away to Annas first; for he was father in law to Caiaphas, which was the high priest that same year. The high priest then asked Jesus of his disciples, and of his doctrine. Jesus answered him, I spake openly to the world; I ever taught in the synagogue, and in the temple, whither the Jews always resort; and in secret have I said nothing. Why askest thou me? ask them which heard me, what I have said unto them: behold, they know what I said. And when he had thus spoken, one of the officers which stood by struck Jesus with the palm of his hand, saying, Answerest thou the high priest so? Jesus answered him, If I have spoken evil, bear witness of the evil: but if well, why smitest thou me?

Then they led him away to Caiaphas the high priest, where the scribes and the elders were assembled. Two false witnesses came, And said, This fellow said, I am able to destroy the temple of God, and to build it in three days. And the high priest arose, and said unto him, Answerest thou nothing? what is it which these witness against thee? But Jesus held his peace. And the high priest answered and said unto him, I adjure thee by the living God, that thou tell us whether thou be the Messiah, the Son of God. Jesus saith unto him, Thou hast said. Then the high priest rent his clothes, saying, He hath spoken blasphemy; what further need have we of witnesses? behold, now ye have heard his blasphemy. *John 18,12; John 18,19 ff.; Matthew 26,57 ff.*

The Trials of Job

There was a man in the land of Uz, whose name was Job; and that man was perfect and upright, and one that feared God, and eschewed evil. Now there was a day when the sons of God came to present themselves before the LORD, and Satan came also among them. And the LORD said unto Satan, Hast thou considered my servant Job, that there is none like him in the earth, a perfect and an upright man, one that feareth God, and escheweth evil? Then Satan answered the LORD, and said, Doth Job fear God for nought? Hast not thou made an hedge about him, and about his house, and about all that he hath on every side? thou hast blessed the work of his hands, and his substance is increased in the land. But put forth thine hand now, and touch all that he hath, and he will curse thee to thy face. And the LORD said unto Satan, Behold, all that he hath is in thy power; only upon himself put not forth thine hand. So Satan went forth from the presence of the LORD.

And there was a day a messenger came unto Job, and said, The oxen were plowing, and the asses feeding beside them: And the Sabeans fell upon them, and took them away; yea, they have slain the servants; and I only am escaped alone. While he was yet speaking, there came also another, and said, The Chaldeans fell upon the camels, and have carried them away, yea, and slain the servants; and I only am escaped alone. While he was yet speaking, there came also another, and said, Thy sons and thy daughters were eating and drinking wine in their eldest brother's house: And, behold, there came a great wind from the wilderness, and smote the four corners of the house, and it fell upon the young men, and they are dead; and I only am escaped alone. Then Job arose, and rent his mantle, and shaved his head, and fell down upon the ground, and worshipped, And said, Naked came I out of my mother's womb, and naked shall I return thither: the LORD gave, and the LORD hath taken away; blessed be the name of the LORD. In all this Job sinned not, nor charged God foolishly.

Job 1,1; Job 1,6 ff.

THE DENIAL OF PETER

Then did the servants spit in his face, and buffeted him; and others smote him with the palms of their hands, Saying, Prophesy unto us, thou Messiah, Who is he that smote thee?

But Peter followed him afar off unto the high priest's palace, and went in, and he sat with the servants. And a damsel came unto him, saying, Thou also wast with Jesus of Galilee. But he denied before them all, saying, I know not what thou sayest. And when he was gone out into the porch, another maid saw him, and said unto them that were there, This fellow was also with Jesus of Nazareth. And again he denied with an oath, I do not know the man. And after a while came unto him they that stood by, and said to Peter, Surely thou also art one of them; for thy speech bewrayeth thee. Then began he to curse and to swear, saying, I know not the man. And immediately the cock crew. And Peter remembered the word of Jesus, which said unto him, Before the cock crow, thou shalt deny me thrice. And he went out, and wept bitterly.

Matthew 26,58 ff.

Cain and Abel

And Adam knew Eve his wife; and she conceived, and bare Cain, and said, I have gotten a man from the LORD. And she again bare his brother Abel. And Abel was a keeper of sheep, but Cain was a tiller of the ground. And in process of time it came to pass, that Cain brought of the fruit of the ground an offering unto the LORD. And Abel, he also brought of the firstlings of his flock and of the fat thereof. And the LORD had respect unto Abel and to his offering: But unto Cain and to his offering he had not respect. And Cain was very wroth, and his countenance fell. And the LORD said unto Cain, Why art thou wroth? and why is thy countenance fallen? If thou doest well, shalt thou not be accepted? and if thou doest not well, sin lieth at the door. And unto thee shall be his desire, and thou shalt rule over him. And Cain talked with Abel his brother: and it came to pass, when they were in the field, that Cain rose up against Abel his brother, and slew him. *Genesis 4,1 ff.*

THE END OF JUDAS

Then Judas, when he saw that he was condemned, repented himself, and brought again the thirty pieces of silver to the chief priests and elders, Saying, I have sinned in that I have betrayed the innocent blood. And they said, What is that to us? see thou to that. And he cast down the pieces of silver in the temple, and departed, and went and hanged himself.

Matthew 27,3 ff.

Moses before Pharaoh

And the LORD said unto Moses, See, I have made thee
a god to Pharaoh: and Aaron thy brother shall be thy
prophet. Thou shalt speak all that I command thee:
and Aaron thy brother shall speak unto Pharaoh, that
he send the children of Israel out of his land. And I
will harden Pharaoh's heart, and multiply my signs
and my wonders in the land of Egypt. But Pharaoh
shall not hearken unto you, that I may lay my hand
upon Egypt, and bring forth mine armies, and my
people the children of Israel, out of the land of Egypt
by great judgments. And the Egyptians shall know
that I am the LORD, when I stretch forth mine hand
upon Egypt, and bring out the children of Israel from
among them. And Moses and Aaron did as the LORD
commanded them, so did they. And he hardened
Pharaoh's heart, that he hearkened not unto them; as
the LORD had said.

Exodus 7,1 ff.

JESUS BEFORE PILATE AND HEROD

Jesus stood before the governor; And when he was accused of the chief priests and elders, he answered nothing. Then said Pilate unto him, Hearest thou not how many things they witness against thee? And he answered him to never a word; insomuch that the governor marvelled greatly.

And as soon as Pilate knew that he belonged unto Herod's jurisdiction, he sent him to Herod, who himself also was at Jerusalem at that time. And when Herod saw Jesus, he was exceeding glad: for he was desirous to see him of a long season, because he had heard many things of him; and he hoped to have seen some miracle done by him. Then he questioned with him in many words; but he answered him nothing. And Herod with his men of war set him at nought, and mocked him, and arrayed him in a gorgeous robe, and sent him again to Pilate. And the same day Pilate and Herod were made friends together: for before they were at enmity between themselves.

And the governor asked him, saying, Art thou the King of the Jews? And Jesus said unto him, Thou sayest. Then Pilate therefore took Jesus, and scourged him. Then the soldiers of the governor took Jesus into the common hall, and gathered unto him the whole band of soldiers. And they stripped him, and put on him a scarlet robe. And when they had platted a crown of thorns, they put it upon his head, and a reed in his right hand: and they bowed the knee before him, and mocked him, saying, Hail, King of the Jews! And they spit upon him, and took the reed, and smote him on the head.

Matthew 27,11 ff.; Luke 23,7 ff.; John 19,1; Matthew 27,27 ff.

Joseph Interprets the Dream of Pharaoh

Then Pharaoh sent and called Joseph, and they brought him hastily out of the dungeon. And Pharaoh said unto Joseph, I have dreamed a dream, and there is none that can interpret it: and I have heard say of thee, that thou canst understand a dream to interpret it. And Joseph answered Pharaoh, saying, It is not in me: God shall give Pharaoh an answer of peace. And Pharaoh said unto Joseph, In my dream, behold, I stood upon the bank of the river: And, behold, there came up out of the river seven kine, fatfleshed and well favoured; and they fed in a meadow: And, behold, seven other kine came up after them, poor and very ill favoured and leanfleshed, such as I never saw in all the land of Egypt for badness: And the lean and the ill favoured kine did eat up the first seven fat kine. And I saw in my dream, and, behold, seven ears came up in one stalk, full and good: And, behold, seven ears, withered, thin, and blasted with the east wind, sprung up after them: And the thin ears devoured the seven good ears. And Joseph said unto Pharaoh, The dream of Pharaoh is one: God hath shewed Pharaoh what he is about to do. The seven good kine are seven years; and the seven good ears are seven years: the dream is one. Behold, there come seven years of great plenty throughout all the land of Egypt: And there shall arise after them seven years of famine; and all the plenty shall be forgotten in the land of Egypt; and the famine shall consume the land; And the plenty shall not be known in the land by reason of that famine following; for it shall be very grievous.

And the thing was good in the eyes of Pharaoh, and in the eyes of all his servants. And Pharaoh said unto his servants, Can we find such a one as this is, a man in whom the Spirit of God is? And Pharaoh said unto Joseph, Forasmuch as God hath shewed thee all this, there is none so discreet and wise as thou art: Thou shalt be over my house, and according unto thy word shall all my people be ruled: only in the throne will I be greater than thou.

Genesis 41,14 ff.

THE CONDEMNATION OF JESUS

Now at that feast the governor was wont to release unto the people a prisoner, whom they would. And they had then a notable prisoner, called Barabbas. Therefore when they were gathered together, Pilate said unto them, Whom will ye that I release unto you? Barabbas, or Jesus which is called Messiah? Whether of the twain will ye that I release unto you? They said, Barabbas. Then released he Barabbas unto them: and when he had scourged Jesus, he delivered him to be crucified.

Matthew 27,15 ff.

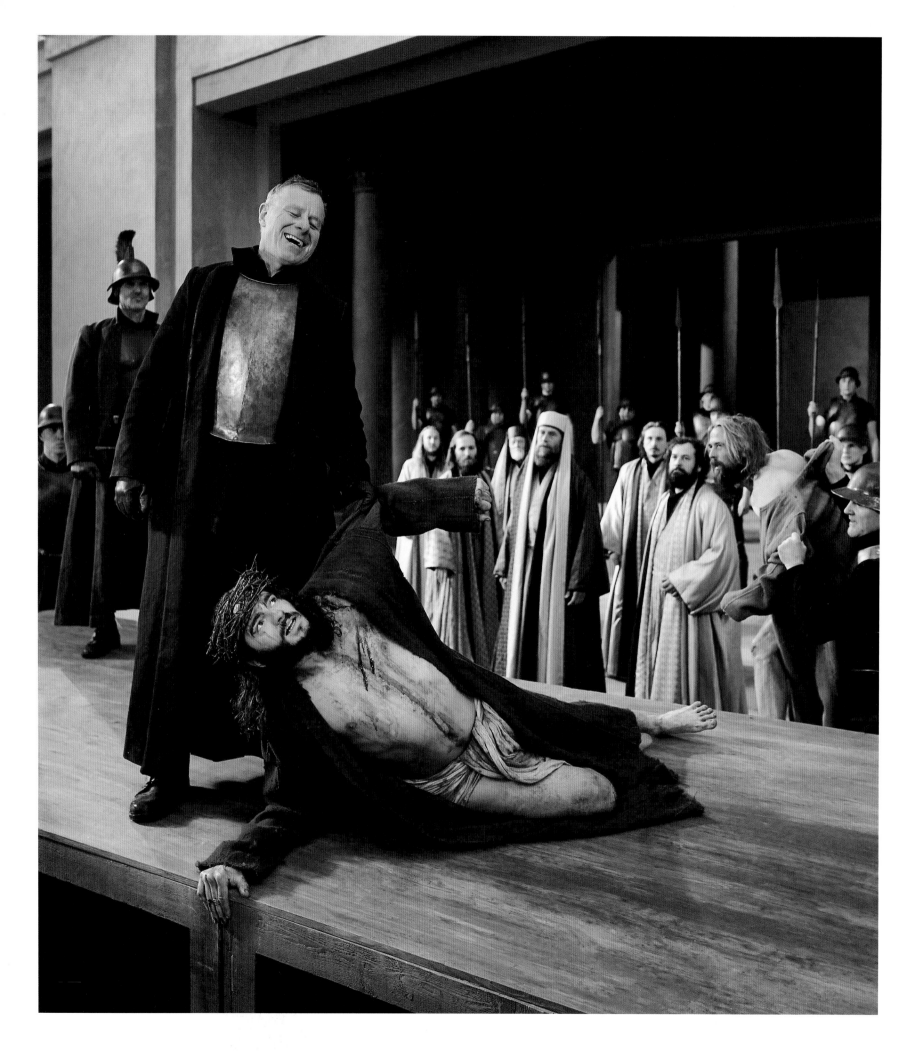

The Sacrifice of Abraham

And it came to pass after these things, that God did tempt Abraham, and said unto him, Abraham: and he said, Behold, here I am. And he said, Take now thy son, thine only son Isaac, whom thou lovest, and get thee into the land of Moriah; and offer him there for a burnt offering upon one of the mountains which I will tell thee of. And Abraham rose up early in the morning, and saddled his ass, and took two of his young men with him, and Isaac his son, and clave the wood for the burnt offering, and rose up, and went unto the place of which God had told him. Then on the third day Abraham lifted up his eyes, and saw the place afar off. And Abraham said unto his young men, Abide ye here with the ass; and I and the lad will go yonder and worship, and come again to you. And Abraham took the wood of the burnt offering, and laid it upon Isaac his son; and he took the fire in his hand, and a knife; and they went both of them together. And Isaac spake unto Abraham his father, and said, My father: and he said, Here am I, my son. And he said, Behold the fire and the wood: but where is the lamb for a burnt offering? And Abraham said, My son, God will provide himself a lamb for a burnt offering: so they went both of them together. And they came to the place which God had told him of; and Abraham built an altar there, and laid the wood in order, and bound Isaac his son, and laid him on the altar upon the wood. And Abraham stretched forth his hand, and took the knife to slay his son.

And the angel of the LORD called unto him out of heaven, and said, Abraham, Abraham: and he said, Here am I. And he said, Lay not thine hand upon the lad, neither do thou any thing unto him: for now I know that thou fearest God, seeing thou hast not withheld thy son, thine only son from me.
Genesis 22,1 ff.

THE WAY OF THE CROSS

And after that they had mocked him, they took the robe off from him, and put his own raiment on him, and led him away to crucify him. And as they came out, they found a man of Cyrene, Simon by name: him they compelled to bear his cross.

And there followed him a great company of people, and of women, which also bewailed and lamented him. But Jesus turning unto them said, Daughters of Jerusalem, weep not for me, but weep for yourselves, and for your children. For, behold, the days are coming, in the which they shall say, Blessed are the barren, and the wombs that never bare, and the paps which never gave suck. Then shall they begin to say to the mountains, Fall on us; and to the hills, Cover us. For if they do these things in a green tree, what shall be done in the dry?

Matthew 27,31 f.; Luke 23,27 ff.

Moses Lifts up the Bronze Serpent

And they journeyed from mount Hor by the way of the Red sea, to compass the land of Edom: and the soul of the people was much discouraged because of the way. And the people spake against God, and against Moses, Wherefore have ye brought us up out of Egypt to die in the wilderness? for there is no bread, neither is there any water; and our soul loatheth this light bread. And the LORD sent fiery serpents among the people, and they bit the people; and much people of Israel died. Therefore the people came to Moses, and said, We have sinned, for we have spoken against the LORD, and against thee; pray unto the LORD, that he take away the serpents from us. And Moses prayed for the people. And the LORD said unto Moses, Make thee a fiery serpent, and set it upon a pole: and it shall come to pass, that every one that is bitten, when he looketh upon it, shall live. And Moses made a serpent of brass, and put it upon a pole, and it came to pass, that if a serpent had bitten any man, when he beheld the serpent of brass, he lived.

Numbers 21,4 ff.

THE CRUCIFIXION AND DEATH OF JESUS

And when they were come unto a place called Golgotha, that is to say, a place of a skull, They gave him vinegar to drink mingled with gall: and when he had tasted thereof, he would not drink. And they crucified him, and parted his garments, casting lots: that it might be fulfilled which was spoken by the prophet, They parted my garments among them, and upon my vesture did they cast lots. And set up over his head his accusation written, THIS IS JESUS THE KING OF THE JEWS. Then were there two thieves crucified with him, one on the right hand, and another on the left. And they that passed by reviled him, wagging their heads, And saying, Thou that destroyest the temple, and buildest it in three days, save thyself. If thou be the Son of God, come down from the cross. Likewise also the chief priests mocking him, with the scribes and elders, said, He saved others; himself he cannot save. If he be the King of Israel, let him now come down from the cross, and we will believe him. He trusted in God; let him deliver him now, if he will have him: for he said, I am the Son of God. The thieves also, which were crucified with him, cast the same in his teeth.

Now from the sixth hour there was darkness over all the land unto the ninth hour. And about the ninth hour Jesus cried with a loud voice, saying, Eli, Eli, lama sabachthani? that is to say, My God, my God, why hast thou forsaken me? Some of them that stood there, when they heard that, said, This man calleth for Elias. And straightway one of them ran, and took a spunge, and filled it with vinegar, and put it on a reed, and gave him to drink. The rest said, Let be, let us see whether Elias will come to save him. Jesus, when he had cried again with a loud voice, yielded up the ghost.

And, behold, the veil of the temple was rent in twain from the top to the bottom; and the earth did quake, and the rocks rent; And the graves were opened; and many bodies of the saints which slept arose, And came out of the graves after his resurrection, and went into the holy city, and appeared unto many. Now when the centurion, and they that were with him, watching Jesus, saw the earthquake, and those things that were done, they feared greatly, saying, Truly this was the Son of God. And many women were there beholding afar off, which followed Jesus from Galilee, ministering unto him: Among which was Mary Magdalene, and Mary the mother of James and Joses, and the mother of Zebedee's children.

Matthew 27,33 ff.

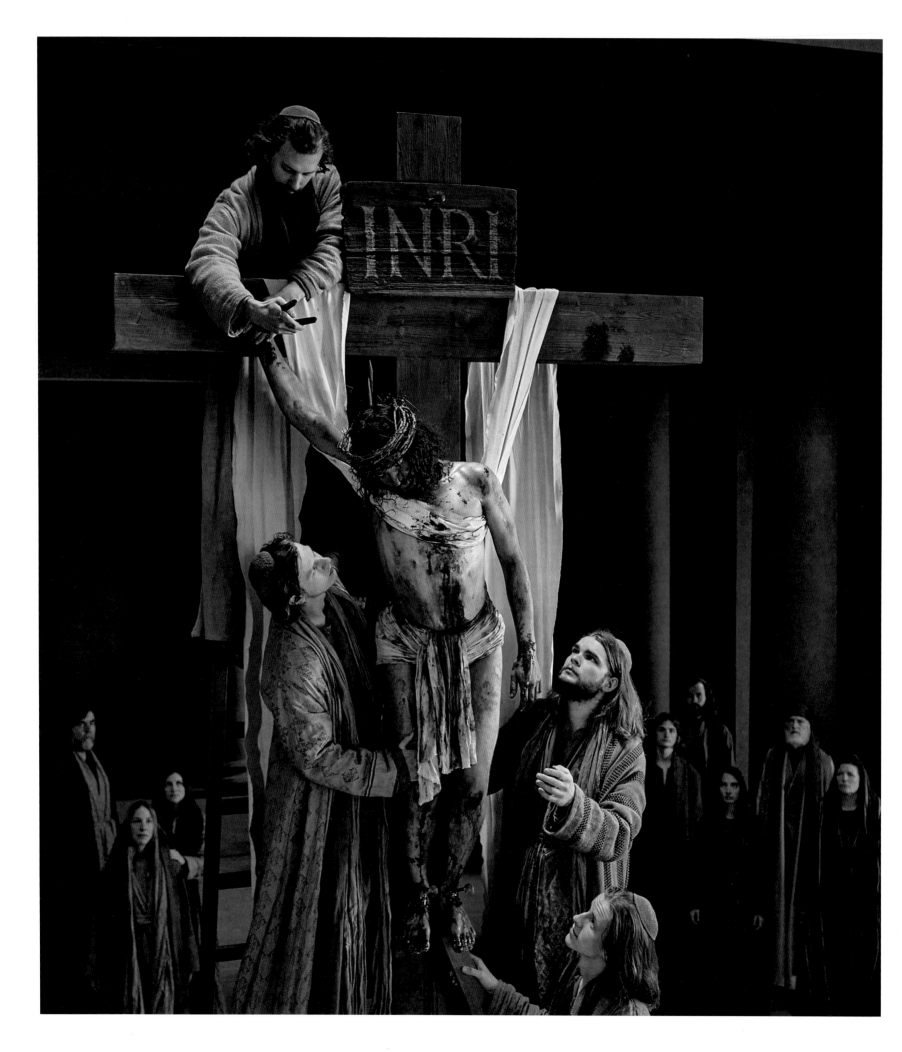

LOOKING BACK AHEAD

Between tradition and transformation they build a bridge to the present day: director Christian Stückl, set and costume designer Stefan Hageneier and musical director and conductor Markus Zwink. A conversation about their work on the Passion Play, moderated by Teresa Grenzmann.

Stefan Hageneier, Markus Zwink and Christian Stückl

Staging, orchestrating and designing the same story over and over again at ten-year intervals – is it a blessing or a curse?

CHRISTIAN STÜCKL (CS): I find it really exciting. It gives you the opportunity to re-examine the story from a completely new perspective. Each reading of the Bible reflects the time in which it's read. You start writing again and you ask yourself, what is important now, what are you focusing on this time? You're never done with this story.

MARKUS ZWINK (MZ): It's interesting when you can change things. I'm interested in the text and how we can bring this big stage to life again and again over five and a half or six hours.

STEFAN HAGENEIER (SH): It's like a serial. You don't invent it from scratch. It is unbelievable what can happen in the world within a decade. But of course the fact that you yourself get older and see other images in it – that's all part of it.

The Passion has been part of your lives since childhood and you've been in charge of the production for over thirty years. How has your attitude towards the play changed from decade to decade?

CS: Between 1970 and 1984 there were constant arguments about the Passion Play. Among the regulars in the pub there was heated debate about the allegations of anti-Semitism, text reform, the involvement of younger Oberammergau residents and, above all, equal rights for women. At some point I had the feeling – that's what I want to do! I realised that if something didn't happen then, it would fall apart. I stood for election together with Markus Zwink, and the municipal council entrusted us to direct the 1990 play. But there was almost nothing we could change in our first year.

MZ: In 1990 I changed seven bars, an instrumental interlude, and even that I had scruples about. We knew that in 2000 we would have to be much more direct.

CS: In 1996 the population elected us for the 2000 play. So the three of us – now including Stefan Hageneier – were more courageous. We said if we're going to do it, we're going to truly reform it.

SH: Even presenting the stage design was a gamble back then. But I approached it with the nonchalance and naivety of youth. I was mainly focused on rejuvenating it aesthetically. My approach certainly wasn't revolutionary, but it was still a surprise to all of us that the concept was so well received.

View of Oberammergau

CS: Instead of a secret ballot, the actors in 2000 were selected by acclamation. But we still had to push every change through the municipal council. For 2010 we said that we weren't going to give them a say in the stage design, and that we also wanted to be free to choose the musicians and actors. The municipal council only had a right of veto. We also pushed through the night play, which means that we now start the performance later and the Crucifixion scene takes place in darkness. That's our mission: to move the Passion Play onwards, take it somewhere new.

Cautious modernisation

Tradition or change – is that basically the question every time?

SH: From professional theatre people I often get the question: "So? Are you going to do a really modern production this time?" Then we have to defend our approach and explain why things are just different in Oberammergau. To date I've never asked myself whether it would be better to show Jesus in modern clothes to make it ostensibly more contemporary. Engaging with the visual world of Christian art history still appeals to me more than superficially transferring it to the modern day. For 2022 I will be presenting images which examine the recurrence of history, which bring history into the now. But you don't need specific contemporary references: the fact that the biblical story continues to unfold in its own timeframe actually makes it more comprehensible in many respects.

CS: It's remarkable – in 1750 the Benedictine pastor Ferdinand Rosner conceived a new structure for the Passion Play, and none of the subsequent writers or directors have ever deviated from this structure. There is an unspoken agreement that the costumes and sets will be in some way historical. That Jesus will be drawn from the material of the Gospels rather than completely reinvented. Naturally a lot of things have changed despite that. We do feel free, but as regards the basic structure we engage with the tradition that has developed over the decades.

On Ash Wednesday 2019, the performers commit to growing out their hair and beards

Jesus actor Frederik Mayet being interviewed

Director Christian Stückl

SH: There is a certain respect, which partly comes from the enormous weight of expectation. If you look at the tableaux vivants, for example, and perhaps wonder if that kind of thing is appropriate anymore, you soon realise they still move the audience and that they're important for the impact of the Passion Play. Tableaux vivants became fashionable in the 18th century and were soon introduced into the Passion Play. So Oberammergau had its finger on the pulse. After Johann Georg Lang's version at the beginning of the 20th century, for a long time there was no new impetus in the Passion Play.

Change or tradition?
Tradition through change!

So changing your own aspirations and perspective is part of it as well?

CS: Naturally the play reflects how we have changed too. You can't just stand still. It is in the nature of our profession to challenge ourselves over and over, to engage with the whole thing over and over.

SH: The seventy years in which they just repeated the same production time and time again didn't do the Passion Play any good. Oberammergau – the home of bad sword-and-sandal theatre? That's all in the past. These days I often read or hear that the Passion Play is perhaps the best example of a certain way of looking at the theatre. It's important that we maintain that.

CS: "Let's preserve things" and "let's change things" – these two approaches have actually been in opposition to each other since the tradition began. The exciting thing is that this friction within the village is ultimately highly significant, it's all part of it.

Hebraic tension in the music

Does the musical development represent a particular challenge here?

MZ: Yes, change is more difficult in the music. So much is text-related, and with new pieces you have to follow the words. Back in 2010 we introduced the scene in which the people sing the "Sch'ma Israel". The shading of the Hebrew language brings a whole new mood to the play. Our intention was to locate Jesus in his Jewish setting so that people would realise that he was not the first Christian, he was simply a product of his time, his land and his environment. And in 2022, the music accompanying the Way of the Cross is not in its usual context. I extracted a few essential phrases From Psalm 22 – "Eli, Eli lama sabachthani" ("My God, my God, why have You forsaken me?"). If we were to suggest dropping the "Heil Dir" or the "Hallelujah", that would be a revolution of course. It's like telling a German not to sing "Stille Nacht" [Silent Night] at Christmas – you just can't do it!

One key innovation for 2022 is that you leave out the prologue speaker, who appeared between the scenes in the play and the tableaux vivants for 200 years. What led to this decision?

CS: Music has always been very important for the people of Oberammergau and for the audience. The tableaux vivants and the music are part of our development. In the very beginning you still had Hell in battle with Heaven. In the first scene, Lucifer would mock the audience. With the tableaux vivants, Hell started disappearing around

Musical director Markus Zwink

Musical rehearsals under pandemic conditions

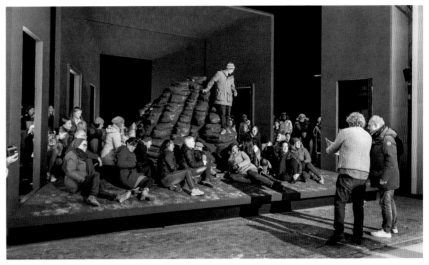

Christian Stückl and Stefan Hageneier block a tableau vivant

1750 or 1780, from the text as well. By dividing it into twelve blocks we are preserving an old form that has now almost completely died out. The music is an integral element of that. But the prologue, which interrupts this music with text, did something that doesn't work any-more: it forced theology on the audience, interpreted the scenes from a post-Easter perspective and kept reminding us we are redeemed by Jesus's death on the Cross. It left no room for individual interpretation and – even worse – it gave the audience a kind of moral sermon to take home with them.

Markus Zwink rehearses with children

Modern devotion –
space for the audience

What is the function of the Old Testament tableaux vivants? What was – and is – the dramatic reason for having them before the scenes of the Passion and death of Christ?

CS: In the original structure of the play, the tableaux vivants were symbolic counter-images to the narrative of Jesus. They were an indi-cation within the text that something from the past was being replaced: Judaism by Christianity. Nowadays we look for the common element. For us, the driving force is to show that God's work has always been in the world. Because Jesus grew up with these Hebraic images, they are his testament, the basis of his actions. In this sense Jesus stands in the tradition of the Jewish prophets; he didn't want to replace the Torah or the commandments of Moses, he wanted to fulfil them. And suddenly the stories that to us seem very far apart, the Old and the New Testa-ment, are seen as directly related to each other.

MZ: Musically, too, the tableaux vivants bring in another level alongside the events of the Passion. They shed more light on the sub-ject, offer an engagement which is intellectual but also emotional, and which ideally has an augmenting effect. It's a similar thing in the Bach Passion, for example, during a chorale when listeners have a moment to pause, to reflect, even to bring themselves into the work if they wish.

SH: From an artistic point of view, the tableaux vivants are devo-tional images. They are concrete situations – but only through their representation as tableaux vivants, frozen at a pivotal moment, do they transcend the concrete. On the one hand they indicate a break, on the other they place the scenes of the play in historical context. You notice quotations from the past while also looking for points of intersection with the present day, without oversimplifying what is going on. And the story of Jesus resonates throughout it all, the realisation that his increasingly cruel Passion makes sense.

Blocking rehearsal for the tableau vivant "The Mocking of Job"

Blocking rehearsal for the tableau vivant "The Humiliation of the Israelites"

The tableaux vivants –
Jesus's inner images

What does that mean for this year's production in particular?

SH: In 2022 the textual aspects are stronger. My approach is to show a large number of people in different variants of oppression and hope – the Old Testament Israelites appear in each tableau vivant as refugees. The basic motif is always the dwelling place; perhaps transformed into paradise or, for Daniel, a dungeon. We are in an intermediate realm between here and there, home and expulsion, protection and persecution. This motif of the exodus makes the story seem totally contemporary. From Jesus's point of view, the tableaux vivants are the images in his mind. On the Mount of Olives, in his hour of greatest need, Jesus confronts himself and his religion. At that moment he draws courage and hope from the images and stories of his Bible, the Torah. This analogy to the narrative of the play is asserted rather than proven, yet it lends another layer of meaning to the play.

Set and costume designer Stefan Hageneier

Two hundred performers
in traditional Oberammergau dress

In the new vow scene at the beginning of the play, you have two hundred members of the choir and the people in traditional Oberammergau dress.

MZ: Yes, the historical Oberammergau figures who appear after the overture serve to document the roots, the origin of the Passion Play.

SH: It's always the costumes that prompt questions about the role of the Passion Play choir. In the past, the choristers were called "guardian spirits" and they tended to wear liturgical vestments. It was looking at old photos that inspired the idea that for 2020 they could be Oberammergau villagers from the time the play was created.

MZ: Musically, the beginning is like a great fermata. The first choral passage is "Lord, you are far away! We are lost" – and the distress of the plague gives rise to the Passion Play in Oberammergau.

Do audiences have to be religious to take something away from the play?

CS: Religious – what does that actually mean? You certainly don't have to belong to a church, no. As a spectator you don't really have to bring anything, you can just turn up. But as a director, if I didn't have the belief and conviction that there is a certain power behind this story, behind this Jesus, I wouldn't be able to tell the story. I wouldn't need to tell it.

SH: As set designer for the Passion Play, I have to confess that it was engaging with Christian imagery that first aroused my interest in the story of Jesus. Nevertheless, a secular point of view is important if you want to even try to deal with it in terms of the drama.

CS: The best thing is when you get the sense that people are rethinking their prejudices and, in engaging with the Passion Play, discovering something that they find interesting, something that moves them.

Telling stories authentically

Is that your motivation for examining the Passion Play over and over?

SH: I think it's right that we tell the story as vividly as possible, that we don't devote so much energy to transferring it to the present day in an obvious manner. Because the message has to come from the story itself. That's what I find theatrical about it.

CS: It's the engagement with the performers that I find important. I enjoy guiding them through the narrative and taking it further. When I was young, I saw how the Catholic Church would send theologians and priests to Oberammergau to give tuition in religious matters in the run-up to the Passion Play. The performers would sit there with a beer upstairs in our tavern listening to some lecture. I did not want that.

Instead, before you start rehearsals you take the lead actors and soloists on a ten-day trip to Israel ...

CS: 2019 was already the fourth time we made the trip to Israel. It's a way for all the lead actors to talk to each other, get to know each other. It forces us to examine the play anew, to ask: what does this have to do with us? When it dawns on the performers how relevant the lines still are, how strong they are, there is a chance that they will then pass that on to the audience.

Christian Stückl at a photo session for the illustrated book

Photographer Birgit Guðjónsdóttir (l.) with deputy director Abdullah Kenan Karaca (third from r.)

Authenticity has become an important keyword in Oberammergau – starting with the costumes.

SH: Yes. For the last two Passion Plays I was searching for old fabrics that convey an authentic character – and they were only available in India. I was there in March 2019 to get the fabrics made using a traditional block print process. There was a carpet and fabric dealer in Istanbul who procured 2,000 square metres of old kilims from Anatolia for Jesus and his companions. For the costume design, there is now an urban realm on one side and on the other a character on a donkey, more rural, poorer – Jesus, who, along with his entourage, riles up a certain social class.

What is the idea behind the set design for 2022?

SH: The objectivity and simplicity of the 1930 stage structure means it is neither one thing or another, it's actually meaningless. Over the past ten years I've added to it again and again and I've taken the liberty of turning it into something completely different. For 2020/22, it felt like a crazy step backwards having to live with this structure when I don't think it's right any more. So I had a very clear idea of investing it with new purpose. I have converted the Passion stage into a sweeping temple complex in which the High Council and the Romans dominate. And along comes someone who is utterly different – an anti-hero. He

The first Passion Play rehearsal on 6 January 2022

clearly represents a provocation – the mere fact that he turns up with a bunch of poor people who really don't fit in. In this situation he must realise that there will be trouble, for this reason alone.

CS: The fact that Jesus enters Jerusalem on a donkey and receives the title "King of Israel" is a rebellion against Rome. It is this insolence that will be the reason for his crucifixion, and the letters INRI on the Cross spell it out: "Jesus of Nazareth, King of the Jews".

A difficult young man

In this year's "Play of the suffering, death and resurrection of our Lord Jesus Christ" you engage more than ever with Jesus the man. What is his socialisation, from the point of view of then and now? Do you see Jesus as a maverick, a nerd, a loner?

CS: I think Jesus was an extremely social person. He had no prejudice regarding background or profession, and he fought against it. He also had a good "crew" around him who really believed that he was the Messiah who could lead the people out of suffering.

MZ: But almost until the end I sense a certain distance between Jesus and everyone else. Over and over you see that his words are not understood, they're not truly accepted, they're reinterpreted, that people ask questions, and sometimes understandably so. To me it makes him seem a little isolated.

CS: The increasing demands of his calling, the increasing commitment on his part, lead to a very difficult idea: if you truly wish to change the world, you have to reckon with your own death.

MZ: That's the crucial phase – and that's precisely why you get the feeling that his followers didn't fully grasp the meaning of his message.

SH: Imagine Jesus preaching like that in today's society. You would see nothing but incomprehension – people would call him crazy! I don't think things were that different back then. I believe that because he took his convictions so far, there were only a few left who truly followed him, who believed his idea that they had to actually follow the path to the end.

The Plague, 2019

Rehearsal for "Expulsion of the Traders"

"Peter" (Martin Güntner) unrolls the Torah

*Identification or irritation –
Messiah or anti-hero?*

What are the limits of the human – and thus the possibility of understanding Jesus on the stage as a human being?

CS: We always see him as the Son of God, but that's a difficult way of looking at him. Jesus is very courageous, even with the priests. Today you would first have to build up that courage. That's where he can be fairly severe. He talks about laws that are made for their own sake. Jesus calls for rebellion. He knows he's making enemies for himself, and he knows that at that time he might be killed for it. But if he were "God", he wouldn't have been sweating blood on the nights leading up to it, when he knew there was no going back. He wouldn't have been so fearful.

What role does God play in the two parts of the Bible? Provocateur?

CS: God doesn't want sacrifices. He says I want your heart, your mind. You have Job there, someone in desperate distress, but ultimately he isn't tempted away from his path to God. And this is precisely the consistency with which Jesus goes to the Cross. It's about human situations in which we find ourselves and how we deal with them. By showing terrible things, the Old Testament is sometimes much closer to us than the New Testament. Humanity itself is to blame for Sodom and Gomorrah, just as it is to blame for climate change now.

Crucifixion rehearsal

Rochus Rückel carries the Cross

A servant of Herod with camel

The last photo before the cancellation of the Passion Play, 2020

Fitting of the Romans' costumes

SH: As such the Old Testament is already describing a process of civilisation. Of course, the context seems enormously archaic.

CS: Often the Old Testament is simply a history book. The Israelites were slaves and that's why they wandered the desert for forty years, because they weren't accepted anywhere, they couldn't settle. First of all, they needed laws. The fact that God gave them the laws is depicted with a lot of bombast, of course, but in the end it is Moses who writes down ten main laws and says if you follow them then almost nothing can really happen to you. And because after forty years they were strong enough to "bring down the walls of Jericho with their trumpets", they took over the land – not because the Lord God said, "Here, take it!"

So can you tell the story of Jesus without God?

CS: Absolutely not. Because God has a meaning in the life of Jesus which determines everything. God is so large, so central in the life of Jesus, it is impossible to separate one from the other. For him there is only one law, which is "Shema Israel": "I am the Lord your God, and if you love me you need no other law. You don't need 'thou shalt not kill', because if you love me, you will not kill."

And the people, in turn, need Jesus as an example of exactly that?

CS: We don't have a God who exerts an influence on our lives – that's what Jesus assumes. Only we can make God's will visible. "I am your hands, your feet, your voice …" Perhaps we could say Jesus was divine in the sense that he lived exactly that, to the utter limit. So God was fully visible in him.

Identification or irritation, Messiah or anti-hero? What is more important to you in this production?

CS: Jesus is not a straightforward figure of identification. He raises questions, he deliberately irritates. A lot of this only emerges during rehearsals, when you notice the tension in the room. The "side notes" are important to me. Like when you read that Jesus is a friend of tax collectors and whores, that he goes to the poor, to the prostitutes, the healing at the Pool of Siloam. Is it really about the religious laws that Jesus supposedly broke? Or is it actually annoyance at the fact that he associated with people who supposedly don't fit into our society, for whom there's no place? And how exactly is that any different now? It isn't, really.

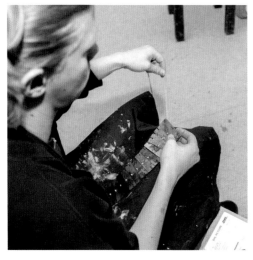
Creating costumes

Constructing columns for the temple

Working on a lion figure

Transport of stage figures

A more human Jesus?
What does that actually mean?

Does the character of Jesus still harbour mysteries for you, despite your close engagement with the story?

CS: You always think, a more human Jesus? Yes. But what does that actually mean? How coarse did Jesus get, how humorous was Jesus, how stubborn was he? It's totally crazy how this character can still puzzle you when you consider how Jesus might react today, at a time when the gap between rich and poor is widening, when there are refugees roaming the world, outcast, a time in which the "love of man grows cold". The most important aspect for me is that Jesus goes to the margins of society, he cares about the marginalised. Perhaps this Jesus that we try to grasp in the Passion Play also has a lot to do with ourselves. That's why it's important that everything Jesus says is anchored in the here and now.

Present the life, not the suffering

So who is Jesus for you in 2022?

CS: The difficult thing about Jesus is the way he is portrayed. When he's too energetic, he almost comes across as a warrior of faith. If he doesn't show humour, he seems arrogant. How far can you go with a character like that on stage, so you feel you are with him all the way? In the rehearsals I got the feeling that Jesus was now becoming a character who despaired of society. And suddenly you don't want humour at all, he shouldn't have to tell jokes – he's all out of jokes.

Do current global political conditions always feed into your thoughts?

CS: We perform the story of Jesus's suffering because of tradition. But in fact we have to act out the story of Jesus's life first. You take it on board, you always have the end in mind, you know he's going to die on the Cross. But why? With every Passion Play you try to make it more political.

MZ: It may be that theatre is always a little bit political. Our play certainly is.

CS: In our present-day society, Jesus has to speak much more clearly and relate to the world. "Why don't you understand my words? Why don't you change?" It's pleading, almost. It reflects Jesus's anger at the world. If we still haven't applied his message after 2,000 years of Christianity, then his mission is a failed mission.

Creating the angels' wings

Susanne Eski prepares costumes

Adjusting a costume

151

The Passionstheater during the rehearsal phase

An intense experience for the audience

Thomas Cook boosted tourism to Oberammergau around 1900. Today there are approximately 500,000 visitors from all over the world. For some, religion is central to their lives. For others, not ...

CS: Theatre was never an end in itself: the audience has always been important. Just a hundred years ago the Passion Play was still a propaganda tool for the church. Even the performer who erected the first stage in our cemetery was a young priest. We know from the Frankfurt Passion Plays in the 14th century that they whipped the audience up against Jews and that there were usually pogroms after the performances. In Oberammergau, the 1934 Passion Play was a propaganda play. But there were also times when the folk drama aspect was more important and people went there to experience "true theatre".

What do you think is important in understanding the biblical characters today?

CS: You're trying to bring about an engagement with the figure of Jesus, to get the audience to discover Jesus anew. But not just him, the figures around him as well. Judas is no longer the "greedy traitor", he's someone who admires Jesus and wants to get him to proclaim himself "King of Israel". Neither the priests nor the people are "unanimous" in their condemnation of Jesus; they are divided into supporters and opponents. Pilate – as is historically documented – turns into a tyrant who has Jesus executed. So the Passion Play is also meant to tear up history and false teachings that have assumed solid form through faith.

Dyeing of thorn bush branches

Photo session for the illustrated book, 2020

Birgit Guðjónsdóttir

World events and amateur theatre

Is it difficult to find over 2,000 participants among the 5,000 villagers?

CS: No, the people of Oberammergau want to perform. But it's difficult to arrange it all because we have to lure people to the Passionstheater for the play, away from their normal jobs. We also always have a rump operation – the management team isn't just the three of us. Certainly we are the ones who come up with ideas in certain areas, but the press spokesman Frederik Mayet, the technical manager Carsten Lück, the head of wardrobe Susanne Eski, the assistants, the other two conductors... If we had to do everything ourselves – hallelujah!

SH: What is difficult is that you have to create a wide range of disciplines from scratch and coordinate them all. What you actually need is the seasoned high-performance operation of a major opera house. But we do now at least have workshops that are as good as any theatre could wish for. It's all highly professional.

It's taken twelve years – finally we are about to witness the postponed première. Is there a moment in the 2022 Passion Play which is particularly special for you?

CS: There isn't one specific scene. I enjoy the people and the shared commitment. My "favourite moment" is working with everyone with whom I put on the Passion Play.

MZ: Me too – it's every moment when I feel that we are getting something back and that the people involved are happy to be together.

Mayor Andreas Rödl and Christian Stückl with the "Hair and Beard Decree"

Actor announcement in front of the Passionstheater on 20 October 2018

SH: For me, the best moment was in 2010, when the whole village came on stage for the very last performance at the end. Because that's what makes the Passion Play so special – it is something that can only happen in the community. It's impossible, but it would actually be good to always do the final scene like that. With everyone singing their lungs out.

The Passion Play keeps Oberammergau together

Would you describe working on the Passion as your life's work?

CS: I think in the end it has become our life's work in a way, yes. Somehow it's part of us. Even if each of us had a completely different starting point in mind. A Passion Play like this only works when you have a strong visual language, the music has plenty of power and the whole thing fits together well with the text. Only then can you really reach people, only then do you create theatre. You need to address all the senses. In the Baroque period they even included odours – they were attempting to capture the human being as a whole.

SH: Ten years is a strange amount of time. But the Passion Play has been around for almost 400 years. It is a grand narrative with grand themes, one that has endured for centuries. As such it will certainly continue.

CS: Here too you can probably trust in the tradition that the Passion Play holds the people of Oberammergau together. Sometimes it was strong, sometimes it was weaker, but it always went on. But as for the future, I'll stick to my old saying: if you want to make God laugh, make a plan!

CHRONICLE

Theatre in the cemetery – the origins of the play (1633–1750)

The history of the Oberammergau Passion Play begins in 1633, in the midst of the Thirty Years' War. With the entry of King Gustav Adolf of Sweden in March 1632, fighting moves to southern Germany and the Bavarian army finds itself battling on its own territory. Augsburg, Landsberg and Munich are all occupied before the Swedish soldiers penetrate into the mountains in June. In his 1850 "History of the Village of Oberammergau", Pastor Joseph Alois Daisenberger describes how they "plundered, pillaged, burned down many houses and villages

head-ache" is carrying inhabitants off as the plague does its furious work. "In the Kohlgrub parish there was such extinction of the populace that only two married couples were to be found there," according to Daisenberger. Oberammergau, however, is spared "through diligent vigil" – until Kaspar Schisler returns home for the autumn church fair on 28 September. The day labourer from Eschenlohe longs to see his wife and children again, but he accidentally brings the Black Death to 84 people in Schisler's village over the next 13 months.

So the legend has it. But the name Kaspar Schisler is nowhere to be found in the Oberammergau death registries. Whoever the actual transmitter of this tragic destiny might have been, in October 1633 the community's overlords

"The Plague Vow", drawing by Hans Schwaighofer

ther plague deaths. And indeed, from then on "not one more person died, although many bore the mark of the plague". It seems unlikely that in 1634 and 1635, when the plague broke out again in Bavaria, there would not have been a single death in Oberammergau – and yet there is no evidence of it.

The first play takes place at Whitsun in 1634 in the Oberammergau cemetery, next to the parish church. Around 60

Bavarian-Austrian region, and by 1800 this number increases more than six-fold to over 250 venues. Also the script with its 4,902 verses – apparently written by a monk from the neighbouring village of Ettal – is not an original but instead largely drawn from two older plays which had been compiled in previous years; this is only discovered in 1880. The two texts are a medieval Passion Play of the second half of the 15th century, a handwritten manuscript of which was found in the Augsburg Benedictine monastery St. Ulrich and Afra, and "On the Tragedy of the Passion and Death/And the Resurrection of Our Lord Jesus Christ" by the Protestant Augsburg Meistersinger Sebastian Wild, which was disseminated around 1566. Presumably the author also drew from a third source which is now lost.

Little is known about the ensuing period up until 1662, which includes the Passion Plays of 1644 and 1654. Daisenberger assumes that the experience of war and disease increasingly turned the people to religion. Two years before the fourth Passion Play year of 1664, the schoolmaster Georg Kaiser produces a copy of the original Oberammergau Passion text. The note "with new amendations" indicates earlier editing.

In 1674 the Oberammergau chaplain Michael Eyrl expands the text with passages from the "Weilheimer Passionspiel", written in 1600 by the parish priest Johannes Älbl. Eyrl is the first named director of the Passion Play. Following the shift to years ending in a zero, the sixth play takes place in 1680.

It is not just the significance of the audience that changes with the end of the 17th and beginning of the 18th century.

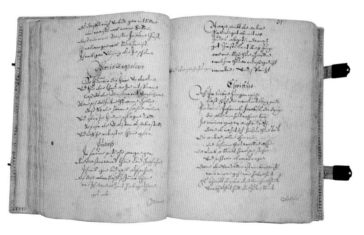

Binding and inner pages of the oldest extant text of the Passion Play, 1662

and inhumanely tormented the inhabitants and killed many of them with cruel blood-lust".

Another mortal danger threatens large parts of the country in 1632 – the "wild

make the decision that from that point on they will perform the "Play of the Passion, Death and Resurrection of our Lord Jesus Christ" every ten years. This pious vow is intended to spare them fur-

to 70 performers perform their parts atop the graves of the plague dead. But in fact this isn't an entirely new tradition: in the period before 1650 there are around 40 Passion Play venues in the

Jesus 1850 Tobias Flunger

1870 Josef Mayr

1890 Josef Mayr

1900 Anton Lang

1922 Anton Lang

1934 Alois Lang

1960 Anton Preisinger

As Oberammergau invests 3,300 guilders in a new parsonage and a schoolhouse, there is the first mention of "expenses due to the Passion Play" in the council accounts. In 1700 the community spends 60 guilders to direct, stage and perform the play, to costume the performers and to provide musical accompaniment. Daisenberger lists in his chronicle: "12 fl. 30 kr. to Bernhard Steinle to conceive and direct the Passion tragedy. 19 fl. to the painters Sebastian Würmseer and Martin Faistenmantel for painting and

There are further text changes under the priest Thomas Ainhaus, who takes over the management and accounting books in 1710, continuing until his death in July 1723. But it is only in the tenth performance year that we see a comprehensive revision. For this the council commissions Father Karl Bader (1662–1731), who has been teaching poetry and rhetoric at the Ettal Ritterakademie since 1713. Surviving parts of his new Passion Play of 1720 mention a Baroque backdrop. But

Father Ferdinand Rosner

As the foundation stone is laid for the lavish Rococo construction of Munich's Cuvilliés Theatre, a replacement for the Residence Theatre destroyed in a fire, at the same time around 90 kilometres away an audience of nearly 11,000 is experiencing a brilliant Baroque spectacle in the Oberammergau cemetery. This becomes the new standard for the Bavarian Passion Play and has numerous imitators. The price for such renown is 88 guilders.

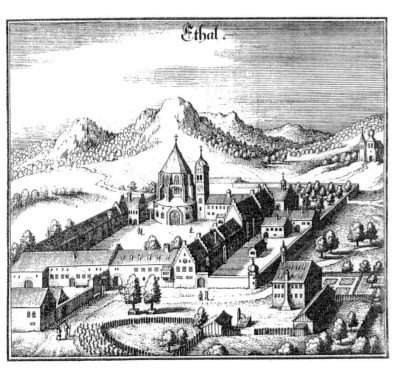

Ettal Abbey in an etching by Matthäus Merian, 1665

paints; 10 fl. to performers paid with one drink as tradition demands; 2 fl. to the trumpeters of Ettal; 12 kr. for powder." The costumes for the performers are lent by the Rottenbuch monastery.

it is not enough to ensure commercial success this time: on conclusion of the play, Oberammergau reports a loss of 73 guilders and 37 kreuzer.

For the 11th performance year of the

Passion Play the prebendary Max Anton Erlböck takes over direction, the first Oberammergau priest to do so. He holds the position for 47 years, until his death in August 1770. There is another revision of the text – and it is by no means insignificant: the Rottenbuch Augustinian monk Anselm Manhart (1680–1752) depicts Jesus in conflict with five adversaries in the form of Satan and the allegorical figures Envy, Avarice, Death and Sin. The council records a deficit of 84 guilders in 1730.

It is another Augustinian monk from Rottenbuch, Clemens Prasser (1703–1770), who revises the text for the performances of 1740 – there are thought to have been two. But it is only the complete reinvention of the Passion Play in 1750 that marks the breakthrough of Oberammergau as a theatre community. Ferdinand Rosner, a Benedictine prior from Ettal and a writer of speeches, poems and (school) plays, writes the village's first dedicated Passion Play text for the 13th performance year: the eloquent, effective "Passio Nova".

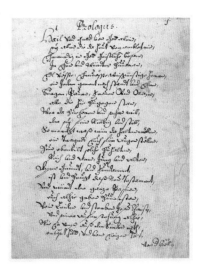

Text of the prologue, 1662

Rosner's new text, encompassing 8,457 verses, places Jesus at the centre of a dramatic struggle between God and the forces of Hell. Continuing on from the previous two performance years, the

1970 Helmut Fischer

1980 Gregor Breitsamter

1984 Max Jablonka

1990 Martin Norz

2000 Anton Burkhart

2010 Andreas Richter

2010 Frederik Mayet

Imagined view of the stage, watercolour, 1780

Minister Maximilian Graf von Montgelas

and other overly realistic portrayals. The plan works: the new Elector Karl Theodor grants the community an exclusive privilege for the performance of the Passion Play. This is renewed for 1790. In the 16th performance year, the Passion Play is mentioned for the first time in a newspaper, while the audience – 11,000 visitors over five performances – are issued with tickets, also a first. The effort pays off, with a profit of 600 guilders.

War is raging in 1800 as Oberammergau receives the privilege of performing the Passion as a "Story of the Passion and Death of Jesus Christ". On 26 June a special performance under military guard is held for soldiers of the Imperial Austrian Army. They hear rhymed verses, see the allegorical figures Pride, Envy and Avarice as well as Lucifer on the cart to Hell. Sixteen days later, on the morning of 12 July 1800, French enemy forces ad-

Elector Maximilian III Joseph of Bavaria

vance on Oberammergau. "Everywhere there was fire, terror, fear and exodus" as the chronicler Daisenberger describes it. "The rectory was soon blazing brightly."

This presages the defeat of Bavaria and Austria at the close of the War of the Second Coalition on 3 December.

After five performances the season is halted. Audiences for the 17th performance year total just 3,000, with a deficit of 205 guilders in the community accounts, offset by four performances in the following year, 1801. Then, on 11 September 1801, the Munich government declares that Oberammergau's privilege has expired.

The advance of secularisation continues. A commission convened on 25 January 1802 by Elector Maximilian IV Joseph is tasked with letting the monasteries and orders slowly die out. Church customs and general portrayals of beliefs are prohibited. Minister Maximilian Count Montgelas forbids the 1810 Passion Play. The community again sends a deputation to Munich. Rejected by the Upper Church Council, Oberammergau turns to the Ecclesiastical Councillor Anton Sambuga with a petition to the king. They only secure the license for the year 1811 through a further concession: another fundamental revision of the Passion Play text.

narrative retains the allegorical figures Envy, Avarice, Death and Sin, as well as Lucifer. One new and noteworthy feature is Rosner's adoption of the Baroque fashion for tableaux vivants. These musical living pictures, which recreate scenes from the Old Testament in a static format, appear at seven intervals during the story of the Passion.

The staging for the 14th performance year of the Passion Play in 1760 appears to have been even more generously appointed. According to the account books the council is down about 156 guilders. There are 14,000 spectators for the two performances.

A dramatic turning point comes on 31 March 1770. Amid a growing wave of secularisation, Bavarian Elector Maximilian III Joseph forbids all Passion

Plays. "The greatest mystery of our holy religion," as he says in his justification, "does not belong on the stage." Oberammergau deputies travel to Munich to request an exemption. To no avail: their appeal is rejected on 22 May and the fate of the Passion Play sealed for the time being. On top of it all, the residents have to bear expenses totalling 274 guilders.

The fact that 1780 is the 15th performance year of the Passion Play is due in no small part to another Benedictine prior from Ettal, Father Magnus Knipfelberger (1747–1825). His text "The Old and New Testament" is an attempt at adaptation. He "cleanses" Ferdinand Rosner's template "of all offensive improprieties", reduces the scenes of Hell to musical interludes and tones down the despair of Judas

Johannes 1870 Johann Zwink

1880 Johann Zwink

1890 Peter Rendl

1922 Melchior Breitsamter

1934 Willy Bierling

1960 Werner Bierling

1990 Robert Heiland

Romanticism –
the search for the original
(1811–1871)

The new play is written by the Ettal Benedictine prior Othmar Weis (1769–1843) who has been working as a teacher in Oberau since the dissolution of the monastery in 1803. Weis focuses on earthly realism, adheres more closely to the Gospels and removes many of the mythological and legendary ele-

Composer Rochus Dedler

ments. And there is no place for the allegorical figures in his prose text. Instead, he inserts Biblical passages and provides current references – moral observations that are preceded by choral passages. Yet he keeps the tableaux vivants. To accompany the performances, the Oberammergau teacher Rochus Dedler (1779–1822), who works

as an organist and cantor in the Rottenbuch monastery until 1802, composes music and revises it repeatedly until 1820. This is the music that can be heard during the Passion Play to this day. He arranges the vocal passages as recitatives, arias and choruses.

The 20th Passion Play is held just four years later due to the end of the Napoleonic wars. As a token of gratitude, eleven special performances are held in 1815. Weis and Dedler add a powerful new large-scale scene, the "Entry into Jerusalem". The revised version also brings a deeper psychological element, in the monologues of Judas, for instance.

For the first time, reports of the performances mention foreign guests: Eugène Rose de Beauharnais (the Duke of Leuchtenberg), adoptive son of Napoleon I, comes with his wife Princess Augusta Amalia Ludovika of Bavaria. And a keen critic of the play makes an appearance: Count Montgelas "was most satisfied by the performance," as Ludwig Clarus recalls in "The Passion Play Of Ober Ammergau" (1860). "With this gentleman's approval of the Passion Play, there was no longer any question of abolishing it."

The next, 21st performance year, 1820, marks a turning point in the history of the Oberammergau Passion. Although the play directed by retired constable G. Luipold is still being produced in the cemetery next to the church – for the last time – it offers an entirely different spectacle. The skilful set construction is devised by the priest Nicolaus Unhoch (1762–1832); Bavarian Royal Architect Anton Baumgartner goes so far as to compare it to Andrea Palladio's Teatro Olimpico in Vicenza. On 25 July he re-

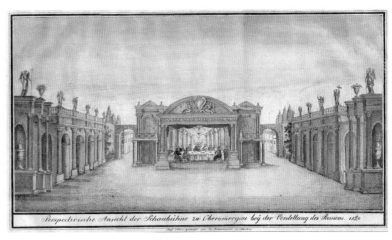

Passion Play set by Nicolaus Unhoch, 1815

cords his recollections of the stage in the *Baierischen National-Blatt*: "It stands on firmly rammed trees, well arranged

"Heil Dir" in the original score, 1815

among themselves through the carpenter's art, while the seats of the audito-

rium are not on boards but also attached to end grain and beam heads. – Anyone who has seen the famous Palladio stage in Vincenza will see some resemblance in the Oberammergau stage, for it presents a square with palaces, gazebos and two broad wings, where the people who are part of the performance may move about freely."

The classicist stage of 1820 decorated with Rococo elements thus already corresponds to the later structure with its wings, the houses of Pilate and the High Priest and the centre stage for the tableaux vivants. The Royal Architect goes into some detail about the psychological portrayal in some of the main roles. The performer playing Christ "seeks to emulate the peace of mind, gravity and humility of his Master", and in Oberammergau, Judas is "neither caricature, nor utterly depraved man".

A municipal bill shows that eight wigs are bought and prepared. Clearly they are not taking the Hair and Beard Decree very seriously at the beginning of the 19th century.

Peter 1870 Jakob Hett

1900 Thomas Rendl

1922 Andreas Lang

1934 Hubert Mayr

1950 Hugo Rutz

1960 Hans Maier sen.

1990 Vitus Zwink

View of the Passion Play stage, 1860

Amalie Lang and High Council member, 1850

The listings printed in the *Münchner politische Zeitung* and in Augsburg newspapers appear to have had the desired effect: audience numbers for the ten performances of the 21st Passion Play amount to around 19,000 in total – twice as many as 1815. At this time the journey from Munich takes two days. The "as-

Sulpiz Boisserée, art historian

sembled crowd of almost 4,000 people paid no mind to bad weather", reports Baumgartner: "For eight hours they were so quiet and attentive that there was not the least interruption."

The success among the public and the press is in inverse proportion to the disappointment of the architect. Nicolaus Unhoch, who was busy building the new stage between October 1819 and Whitsun 1820, is paid poorly for his work. In his diary he notes: "Several theatre connoisseurs from Munich and Augsburg praised the theatre highly,

although the Ammergauers were not very happy with it."

Still, Unhoch returns to design the set for the next play in 1830. Perhaps it is the new venue on the north-western edge of the village, on the "Passion Meadow", that appeals to him. It is a matter of conjecture whether this change results from a prohibition by King Ludwig I or the local pastor Alois Plutz. The chronicler Daisenberger speaks of lively previews, "the fame of the Ammergau Passion Play spreading widely throughout Germany as the lone relic of the old mystery play." Yet although the new fenced-in auditorium can accommodate 5,000, only about 13,000 come to the eleven performances, which has a cast and crew of around 300.

This is the last year for some time that the organisers will need to worry about audience numbers, a fact indirectly attributable to the writer Johann Wolfgang von Goethe, then 81 years old. In 1830 he

Joseph Alois Daisenberger

publishes the admiring judgement of art historian Sulpiz Boisserée in the private journal *Chaos*: "Not only was everything presented earnestly and respectfully [...], the plan of the whole production was so unique, arranged with such intelligence and artistry, that I could not fail to admire it, and often did one feel edified and inspired."

From 1840 onwards this is echoed by the romanticising judgements of other well-known reviewers, such as Guido Gorres and Martin Deutinger, while the English merchant Joseph Brooks Yates writes the first report in English. With the plays in Mittenwald and Kohlgrub discontinued, the community buys their costumes and establishes a permanent store of props and a wardrobe.

Among the 35,000 visitors in this 23rd performance year are Crown Prince Maximilian of Bavaria, Friedrich Au-

Crown Prince Maximilian of Bavaria

Maria Anna of Bavaria

King Friedrich August II of Saxony

gust II King of Saxony and his wife Archduchess Marie Caroline of Austria. Munich coachmen bring guests from Munich to Oberammergau with an overnight stay in Murnau. Departure is at 6 a.m., arriving at the Passion Theatre two days later in time for the start of the play at 8 a.m.

For the 24th Passion Play performance year in 1850, Joseph Alois Daisenberger, pastor of Oberammergau since 1845, takes over direction of the play. He confines his editing of the text to "changing some expressions that are outdated, too coarse or too weak and shortening some speech that is too spun out". For the first time, the organisation of the play is entrusted to a "Passion Committee" made up of elected men and the municipal ad-

ministration. Some of the 464 participants – actors, singers and musicians – receive lessons in advance of the Passion. The stage is rebuilt based on the old model, and some of the costumes restored. The oldest surviving photograph of the Passion Play is created using the Munich Steinheil process; it shows the

actor playing Jesus, Tobias Flunger, in a white, toga-like robe.

From 20 May to 15 September there are twelve performances, then two more, and on 30 September a further performance for Queen Marie of Bavaria. Daisenberger tells of visitors from Berlin, Hanover, Erfurt, Dresden, Prague, Bolzano, Zurich and Geneva – 45,000 in total. Queen Sophie of Bavaria is also among the guests this year, as well as a twelve-year-old noblewoman by the name of Elisabeth, Duchess in Bavaria, later the Austrian Empress "Sisi". The community gives 6,500 guilders from the profits of the Passion Play to charity, and 10,000 guilders to the participants. Following his visit in 1850, the well-known theatre director Eduard Devrient,

Copperplate of the Passionstheater, 1860

After the first visitors from Britain in 1870 – including banker Leopold de Rothschild and Crown Prince Albert Edward, the future King – on 25 September 1871 King Ludwig II of Bavaria attends a private performance of the Passion Play. The auditorium, still open to the elements at the time and able to hold audiences of up to 10,000, on this occasion hosts just the King and his four companions. Two days later at his Schloss Linderhof residence, he receives the performers who play Christ and the apostles. The King hands each a silver spoon – except "Judas", Georg

The Crucifixion Group

Passion Play that he gifts the community with the marble sculpture on the Osterbichl known as the Crucifixion Group, at that time the largest stone monument in the world, weighing 116 tons.

König Ludwig II. von Bayern

who at the time is writing his "History of the German Dramatic Arts", asks what art can learn from the Oberammergau amateur theatre – which he finds to be a synthesis of festival, folk drama and

worship. German-language newspaper articles are soon joined by reports in French and English. But this era also sees increasingly anti-Semitic interpretations of the play.

The thorough revision of the Passion Play text that Daisenberger produces in the run up to the play of 1860 is made largely at the government's request. He draws primarily from the Gospel of John and emphasises universal qualities. Politics gives way to psychology, at the same time leaving more space for idealisation, richness of imagery and folklore (legends, the Way of the Cross). There are 100,000 visitors for the total of 21 performances.

Ten years later Daisenberger writes a Passion in blank verse, but the community rejects this draft. On 17 July 1870 the war against France is announced from the stage during the prologue. The 26th play can only be resumed in 1871.

View of the Passion Play stage, 1870

Lechner, who receives a tin spoon. The "Kini", as the Bavarians call their king, is so delighted with the performance of the

For the first time, a kind of star cult develops around a Christ actor: Josef Mayr. A photographer from the town of

Mary 1870 Franziska Flunger

1880 Anastasia Krach

1890 Rosa Lang

1900 Anna Flunger

1922 Marta Veit

1930 Anni Rutz

1984 Ursula Burkhart

Last Supper, 1870

shortening the journey from Munich. Package tourism finds fertile ground in the Ammer Valley.

Austrian author Ferdinand Groß recalls "an invasion from Frankfurt to Murnau" in his "Oberammergau Passion Letters", and claims that "Englishmen would buy tickets for Judgement Day itself." "The 'Christ' Mair has 50–60,000 'friends'

Auditorium stand 1880

Play at Oberammergau" he praises the production but finds fault with the composition and execution: "The deeper the spectator is captured in his heart, the lustier and more banal the music, and the listener is injured and insulted, the dramatic effect destroyed." For the first time, the orchestra occupies the pit.

Despite the huge audience of 1880, there is now great uncertainty regarding the implementation of the new stage planned for 1890, and the investment of 12,000 to 14,000 marks for new garments, made by the Munich Court Theatre, is now at stake. For the town is deeply in debt. Ultimately the search for a lender

Weilheim, J. Steigenberger not only captures the main actors on camera, but also the stage and the tableaux vivants. But is it theatre or an act of public worship? The Dresden literary scholar Adolf

a 17-year-old actress. She is one of almost 700 performers.

In the same year Thomas Cook travels to Oberammergau and boosts international tourist flow. Travel writers from

visiting him. His etchings are like relics; the Englishwomen want to have them blessed by the Pope in Rome."

Among visitors, too, the huge crowds in the small town arouse more than merely solemn sentiments. In his 1881 travelogue "A Glance at the 'Passion Play'", the British explorer Richard Burton advises gaining "all the 'edification' you may" from the Passion Play but then leaving the place "as fast as you can", so as not to "breed a madness in the brooding brain". The Swabian composer Cyrill Kistler criticises the inappropriate "fairground mood" of the audience. In his publication "The Passion

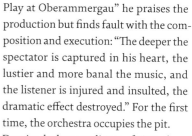

Carl Lautenschläger

Stage, 1880

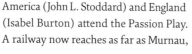

Garden festival at the Passionstheater, c. 1890

Stern responds at the time in the *Dresdner Journal*: "It is the utmost folly to say that the Ammergau Passion Play is an act of public worship and not [at the same time] a theatrical performance! [...] In truth, the great spiritual play is and remains a dramatic representation of the utmost solemnity, the deepest consecration, the purest and innermost elevation. These are attributes accorded all serious artworks in the highest sense, and that includes, but never excludes, a striving for artistic perfection!"

The Passion Play now draws spiritual and secular notables, writers and artists. Among the 100,000 guests in 1880 are Queen Victoria of Sweden, Sergei Alexandrovich Romanov, son of Tsar Alexander II, and the Prussian Crown Prince Friedrich Wilhelm. On 22 August the Emperor's organist, Viennese composer Anton Bruckner, falls in love with

America (John L. Stoddard) and England (Isabel Burton) attend the Passion Play. A railway now reaches as far as Murnau,

The tableau vivant, "Expulsion from Paradise", 1890

results in a strict separation of community and Passion funds. As a further innovation, the Catholic pastor receives a seat and a vote on the Passion Play Committee. The plans of the internationally renowned Munich theatre technician Carl Lautenschläger are ambitious, with the stage receiving a neo-Renaissance facade, the side houses now separate and the boxes and seats brought under cover. Naturally, Lautenschläger modernises the technical equipment as well. For this new production, with its naturalistic, historicist features, he illuminates the centre stage and makes possible spectacular effects such as rapid changes and angel wings.

The play is now world-famous. Among the 124,000 spectators at the 40 performances are Thomas Joseph Carr, Archbishop of Melbourne, Queen Isabella II of Spain, the Sultan of Johor, Malaysia, and the painter Franz von Lenbach.

Construction of the auditorium, 1899

Jesus departs from Mary, 1900

In preparation for the turn-of-the-century Passion the community takes out a loan of 140,000 marks to build an auditorium with 4,200 seats – an iron-frame construction with six arches and a wooden saddle roof. Perhaps it is this impressive theatre basilica that attracts Gustave Eiffel, who arrives from Paris during the 29th year of the Passion Play. And in the same month that the LZ 1 airship makes its first test flight over Lake Constance, Count Ferdinand von Zeppelin witnesses a very different spectacle in Oberammergau.

During the performances of 1900, the coins found in the church offertory come from Egypt, India, Hong Kong, the US, Mexico, Brazil, Bolivia and Peru. The oil magnate John Davison Rockefeller visits from New York. The village is overwhelmed but prepares – an "accommodation office" has been set up and an "arrangement" offers tickets with accommodation included.

The production of souvenirs begins. The most popular motif for postcards and

Stage and auditorium, 1900

autograph photos is the 25-year-old potter Anton Lang. In 1900 he plays Christ before 174,000 spectators, in 1910 it is as many as 223,548 and in 1922 around 311,000, a third of them from abroad. Following his visit, Rabbi Joseph Kraus-kopf publishes the essay "A Rabbi's Impressions of the Oberammergau Passion Play" in the US. In it he describes the harmony of the play and the life of Oberammergau, noting that "the village has the appearance of a bit of Judea transplanted into the heart of the Bavarian Alps". But he also criticises the anti-Semitism in the play and stresses that preaching, teaching and performing a story that incites passions and prejudices resulting in false hatred is unchristian, and injurious to peace and good will.

When the 500-seat "Nogglhaus" opens on Schnitzlergasse on 31 July 1901, Oberammergau finally gains a rehearsal theatre. On 29 November the council decides to introduce a Play Law for 1910. With the population steadily growing, participation is only open to those "who have been resident in the community since 1900 and were involved in the municipal theatre in the nine intervening years".

In its 30th year, shortly before the First World War, the Passion Play has an unpa-

Passionstheater with view of the Laber, 1900

ralleled mass impact. Aristocrats, bishops, politicians and artists come to the Ammergau region in 1910, including Cardinal Achille Ratti, later Pope Pius XI, King Gustav V of Sweden, British Prime Minister David Lloyd George and American President William H. Taft, the composer Richard Strauss, the painter Olaf Gulbransson and the writer Hugo von Hofmannsthal. Theatre director Max Reinhardt is greatly impressed by the impact of the Passion Play, which finds an echo in his concept for the Salzburg Festival.

By contrast, writer Lion Feuchtwanger is horrified, as he confides in an essay for *Die Schaubühne*. He describes the Passion Play as a "changeling, begat by the language of the Gospels and a country clergyman striving for a spasmodic formal German rather than his familiar dialect". For him, the Jesus of Oberammergau is "a highly uninteresting figure who upsets himself at the trivial, indulges in the incomprehensible and insignificant, while conducting himself like a lamenting headmaster".

The Oberammergau Play is overshadowed by the First World War, with many actors and musicians severely wounded or killed. In 1918 the Passion Play for 1920 is cancelled.

Caiaphas 1850

1870 Johann Lang

1890 Johann Lang

1930 Hugo Rutz

1960 Benedikt Stückl

1990 Walter Fischer

2000 Stephan Burkhart

The Passion Theatre
in the Third Reich
(1921–1970)

On 21 March 1921, Oberammergau votes in favour of staging a Passion Play in 1922. The 33-year-old sculptor Georg Johann Lang is appointed director. Visitors in the 31st performance year include Nuncio Pacelli, later Pope Pius XII, and Herbert Hoover, later President of the United States. They are joined by German writer Joachim Ringelnatz and the composer Giacomo Puccini, who often visits Germany in his later years in search of new musical and theatrical inspiration.

The tableau vivant "Ascension", 1930

Director Georg Johann Lang and his brother, the mayor Raimund Lang

The effect of the unexpected crowds is not felt in the accounts: the revenue of 19,752,916 marks is consumed by inflation. Catering to the Passion Play visitors devours enormous sums. There are calls for a boycott and even threats of violence. Despite the criticism, the community remains committed to its vow. One key argument against cancelling the play is competition: since the turn of the century,

Europe has seen an increasing number of new plays modelled on Oberammergau, with the Passion Play enjoying a veritable renaissance after World War One.

The town rejects numerous film offers from home and abroad, despite the financial temptation; indeed, it is not until 2010 that a complete recording of the Oberammergau Passion is made. In August 1933 the community turns to direc-

Last Supper, 1922

tor Luis Trenker, but he soon cancels. Yet it is not the Passion Play that they wished to see filmed, but the background story – "The Plague Disaster Anno 1633" by Leo Weismantel – which is performed in the Kleines Theater for the first time to mark the 300th anniversary. Carefully revised by Martin F. Wall in 1998 and again by Christian Stückl since 2009, "The Plague: The Play of the Oberammergau Passion Vow" is still today staged in the year preceding the Passion Play.

For the 32nd performance year, 1930, Georg Johann Lang has in mind not just a fundamentally new production with powerful mass scenes, but also a rebuilding of the stage, unadorned and monumental. He provides the designs for this himself, along with his brother, government architect Raimund Lang. In addition, the auditorium is expanded by adding an iron arch and now offers space for 5,280 guests. Among the 380,000 visitors for the 81st performance are Henry Ford, Indian Nobel Literature Prize winner Rabindranath Tagore and physicist Max Planck. On 21 July, Adolf Hitler is in the audience with his niece Geli Raubal and Joseph Goebbels. Goebbels sees in Oberammergau the "origin of the

German tradition" and for Hitler it is almost an instructional work. He declares Pilate to be the prototype of the "racially and intellectually" superior Roman, who "appears like a rock in the midst of the Jewish dregs and crowds".

Hitler returns to the Passion Theatre on 13 August 1934, together with a number of Nazis, joining audiences for a special season to mark the 300th anniversary. It is dominated by the Nazis of Oberammergau and the new regime, with posters from the village, which has just 3,000 or so residents, declaring "Germany is calling you!" Ticket and admission prices are halved. On 19 December 1933 the minutes of the Passion Committee, now all members of the Nazi Party except

Poster for the 1934 anniversary play

Pastor Bogenrieder, record deliberation on ways that the play can be "kept clean" and protected "against foreign elements". But much like the upcoming Olympic

Guests, 1930: Automotive pioneer Henry Ford

Nobel Prize winner Rabindranath Tagore

Guests, 1934: actress Marion Davies

Adolf Hitler

"American in tribal costume"

Cardinal Michael von Faulhaber

Jean-Paul Sartre and Simone de Beauvoir

Mayr family, 1934

Heinzeller family, 1950

Hochenleitner family, 1960

Müller family, 1960

Lang family, 1960

Stückl family, 1970

Schuster family, 1980

Winter Games in Garmisch-Partenkirchen in 1936, the international event has to offer a pretence of racial tolerance. Hitler declares the play "important to the Reich". Raimund Lang, who has joined the National Socialists and been appointed the new mayor of Oberammergau, finds

Luggage porters, 1950

a kindred spirit to serve as patron in Bavarian Economics Minister Hermann Esser. He declares that "the new Germany" is "a land of prosperity, peace and order". And this impression is not refuted by the contingent of foreign correspondents. For the anniversary play there is an international audience of unprecedented

Bekanntmachung

Das Passionsspielkomitee ruft die mitwirkungsberechtigten Männer auf, sich ab 15. Februar 1959 Haar und Bart wachsen zu lassen. - Die ziviltragenden Mitwirkenden, die diesem Aufruf nicht nachzukommen brauchen, werden in Kürze vom Passionsspielkomitee für ihre Aufgabe im Spiel 1960 bestellt.

Oberammergau, den 12. Februar 1959

Das Passionsspielkomitee
LANG

Hair and Beard Decree, 1959

breadth among the 410,000 spectators; King Prajadhipok, Rama VII of Siam, media tycoon William R. Hearst – but also Simone de Beauvoir and Jean-Paul Sartre. Later, in her autobiography "In the Prime of Life", the philosopher enthuses about the pull of the performance, the truth in the play and the performers' great powers of persuasion. "We didn't have much of a taste for folkloric performances, but the Passion was truly great theatre."

In the run up to the 1940 play, Mayor Raimund Lang decides that proposals for actors and musicians will now be dis-

Last Supper, 1960

cussed within the Party. But the Second World War thwarts these plans and for the second time in its history the Passion Play is not staged.

Because of the high number of refugees and evacuees, the population of the village increases by more than two thirds after the war. In addition to the 60 approved "sales huts", the municipality builds 15 more itself and leases them to the new citizens. The German Federal Railways invests 700,000 DM in the renovation of the station and to extend the platform. And rather than six buses travelling from Garmisch to Oberammergau, there are now 40.

For the 34th performance year, the state government of Bavaria grants the municipality a loan of one million Deutschmarks. There are 33 performances planned for 1950, but even so audience numbers reach a surprising new high – around 480,000. A further 54 performances are planned, and the loan is soon paid off. For each performance, 820 paying tickets are reserved for members of the American and British occupying forces.

Only a few well-known politicians number among the guests: West Germany's President Theodor Heuss and its Chancellor Konrad Adenauer, as well as US President Dwight D. Eisenhower. The Archbishop of Munich and Freising, Michael Cardinal Faulhaber, is also present. Later he will resist calls for a quick repetition of the play the following year, coming down on the side of tradition.

The Oberammergau composer Eugen Papst arranges Rochus Dedler's Passion Play music. The production remains the same as it was before the war. In 1949 the American Jewish Committee (AJC) submits a list with requests for changes, but director Georg Johann Lang explains: "We have a clear conscience. We have to fulfil a vow and there is nothing offensive in our play." Jewish intellectuals, such as the composer Leonard Bernstein and the playwright Arthur Miller, see the matter

Postcard, 1960

differently. They launch a petition to oppose what they see as the play's anti-Semitism, its stereotypical, negative portrayal of Jews. Only on 15 August 1949 does the American military government give the go-ahead for the 34th Passion.

The criticism doesn't let up in the following years, either. Leo Weismantel,

The tableau vivant "Adam works by the sweat of his brow", 1970

The tableau vivant "Expulsion from Paradise", 1970

Toward the present day –
a new generation
(1977–2022)

author of the plague play, says in the *Frankfurter Allgemeine Zeitung* in 1960: "As a written work, the Oberammergau text is extremely primitive; it belongs to the category of devotional literature and cannot be discussed in the context of 'poetry'". On 27 May Johannes Jacobi writes in *Die ZEIT*: "In future, Oberammergau can only justify the global interest that it enjoys every ten years […] with a new version of the play." For 1960, Lang is looking for a new author. Ultimately, however, he returns to the 1930 staging for the 35th performance year, with small changes by Abbot Johannes M. Hock from Ettal, performed in front of half a million people.

After the performance an "advisory body on the issue of a revised text of the Oberammergau Passion Play" is convened. This body decides to use Father Ferdinand Rosner's "Passio Nova" from 1750. This suggestion comes from Carl Orff and the sculptor Hans Schwaighofer,

the designated director. Orff is also to compose the music.

By 1966 preparations are ready: Schwaighofer presents the Rosner text as well as the production and set designs to the council. But the council decides on an adaptation of the Weis/Daisenberger drama instead. Schwaighofer resigns. The new director for 1970 is the hotelier Anton Preisinger, the Jesus of the Passion Plays of 1950 and 1960. Julius August Cardinal Döpfner, Archbishop of Munich and Freising, and the New York Rabbi Marc H. Tanenbaum call for a rethink. The Cardinal withdraws the church mandate, the "Missio canonica", for the play. While Jewish organisations in the United States boycott the play and return about 5,000 tickets, Oberammergau breaks its visitor record again in its 36th year, with over 530,000 spectators at 102 performances.

The eight performances in 1977 see 700 Oberammergau residents take part. The "Rosner Rehearsal" is the result of an intensive process which the municipality entrusts to Hans Schwaighofer (staging, design), Alois Fink (text) and Wolfgang Fortner (music). Their new response to the controversy is very well received by the public and critics. But even in 1980 the community is still not ready to break away from the old play; the majority of citizens vote against the Rosner text.

Hans Schwaighofer rehearses with "Judas", Peter Stückl

For the 37th performance year, the sculptor Hans Maier takes over direction of the Passion. Small corrections are made to the text based on proposals for a more positive view of Judaism presented by the American theologians Svidler and Sloyan in 1978 on behalf

of the Anti-Defamation League, and the sets are redesigned. One eyewitness is Cardinal Ratzinger, later Pope Benedict XVI, who gives the play his ecclesiastic blessing in advance. For the first time, the 18 main roles are cast with two actors of equal status; some protagonists of the Rosner Rehearsal refuse to take part. Audience numbers total around 460,000, a drop attributed to the reduction of seats in the auditorium to 4,700.

The community welcomes around 480,000 spectators to the 350-year celebration four years later in 1984, among them the minister-presidents of Bavaria and Baden-Württemberg Franz Josef Strauss and Lothar Späth. Women who take part in the play are now permitted to sit on the Passion Play Committee. But except for a few amendments to the text and some transformations of the set there is no fundamental reform for the 38th year of performance.

On the advice of the Archbishop of Munich, Cardinal Friedrich Wetter, the new council convenes a Text Commission that same year under the leadership of theologian Rudolf Pesch, which is mainly concerned with the proposals of the Americans Svidler and Sloyan. In the summer of 1986, the 27-year-old sculptor Christian Stückl is elected director in a very close vote. Otto Huber, a high school teacher, becomes the deputy director. The pair's first official act is to revise Pesch's text version once again. Despite conflict within the committee, many anti-Jewish passages are dropped. This new text is still based on the Daisenberger original but the revision also reflects new exegetical, theological

The tableau vivant "The Bronze Serpent", 1990

The tableau vivant "The Bride", 2000

The tableau vivant "Dance around the Golden Calf", 2010

Christian Stückl and "Jesus", Frederik Mayet

and historical findings. At the same time, the new musical director Markus Zwink revises and expands Rochus Dedler's composition.

For the casting in April 1989, Stückl insists that a third of the main roles be filled by actors under 30. The 19-year-old actor Carsten Lück is the first Protestant to play a major role. Previously, married women and women over 35 were excluded from participation in the Passion Play. But on 22 February 1990, three women from Oberammergau go to court for their right to perform. More than 250 actresses are subsequently integrated into the staging. For the first time in the history of the Passion Play, a married woman plays the role of Mary. Protests against these changes see 18 lead actors and extras resign.

The Crucifixion, 2000

Inspired by Cardinal Friedrich Wetter and Christian Stückl, the actors, vocal soloists and director begin a new tradition: led by a Jesuit and joined by local clergy they prepare for the Passion Play by undertaking a ten-day trip to Israel. Audiences totalling 480,000 come to the 98 performances in the 39th performance year of 1990, among them Ger-

man President Richard von Weizsäcker and Bavarian Minister-President Max Streibl.

A public petition on 14 May 1996 calls for the re-election of Christian Stückl as director. The vote on 29 September finds 55.2 percent of the Oberammergau population in favour of Stückl. At the same time this signals approval for the greatest reform of the Passion Play since 1860. Once again Otto Huber assumes the position of deputy director and dramaturge. They are joined by a theological advisor in the form of Ludwig Mödl.

The actors' trip to Israel, 2019

The new version of the text for the year 2000 lends greater individuality to the role of Jesus. As a strong fighter for his faith, he is at the centre of an internal Jewish conflict, finding both advocates and adversaries on the High Council, among the ordinary people and in the ranks of his followers.

In addition to the new arrangement of the music of 1811/15, Markus Zwink composes music for the new tableaux vivants that replace the ones removed from the play because of their anti-Jewish content. The 27-year-old Stefan Hageneier designs the first new set in decades. Twenty-eight scenes and almost 2,000 costumes are created for the 1,600 adults and 550 children of the 110 performances of the 40th Passion Play. Muslim Oberammergau residents take part for the first time. Among the 520,000 enthusiastic visitors are German President Roman Herzog, Bundestag Speaker Wolfgang Thierse and the Bavarian Minister-President Edmund Stoiber, as well as the American artist Robert Wilson and Turkish writer Feridun Zaimoglu.

Service to mark the renewal of the vow, 2018

For the 41st year in 2010, Christian Stückl makes more fundamental changes to the Passion text, while Otto Huber writes new text for the tableaux vivants to forge a link with the present day. For the first time, the play extends into the evening hours; the Crucifixion scene now takes place in darkness.

The aim is to show the persona of Jesus Christ, the querulous young Jew. The music now takes on a greater role in the narrative. Markus Zwink creates powerful tension with choral passages in Hebrew, such as the "Sch'ma Israel" during the Cleansing of the Temple, and certain chord combinations that create a Middle Eastern sound. This, too, locates Jesus in his Jewish context. Using poetry, colour and symbolism, Stefan Hageneier crafts bright, modern devotional images in a powerful aesthetic idiom. Another new addition is the mobile stage roof, designed by the architects Jabornegg & Pálffy.

German Chancellor Angela Merkel, President Christian Wulff, Cardinal Reinhard Marx, Archbishop of Munich and Freising, and the New York Archbishop Cardinal Timothy Michael Dolan are among the 515,000 guests for the 2010 Passion, in which 2,400 Oberammergau residents participate in a total of 109 performances.

In 2015 the municipal council once again entrusts the direction of the next Passion Play, 2020, to the team led by Christian Stückl, Stefan Hageneier and Markus Zwink. The young Oberammergau resident Abdullah Kenan Karaca is appointed deputy director.

On 14 March 2020, two months before the premiere, rehearsals are shut down due to the corona pandemic. Five days later, the 42nd Passion Play is officially postponed by two years. A strange coincidence: in 1920, exactly one hundred years earlier, the play was cancelled and postponed by two years. And, of course, it was a pandemic – the plague itself – that led to the very first Oberammergau Passion story almost 400 years earlier. The 425,000 tickets already sold for 2020 are rebooked or cancelled.

But on 5 October 2020 presales begin again, and stage rehearsals resume in early 2022. There is a greater focus than ever on the question of how the Passion Play can better reflect current themes. "And vice versa," says Christian Stückl. "All the problems we have today appear in the Passion story as well."

Teresa Grenzmann

The Passionstheater, 2022

ACTORS

JESUS

Frederik Mayet   Rochus Rückel

PETER

Martin Güntner   Benedikt Geisenhof

JOHN

Anton Preisinger   Christoph Stöger

JUDAS

Martin Schuster   Cengiz Görür

MARY

Andrea Hecht   Eva-Maria Reiser

MARY MAGDALENE

Barbara Schuster   Sophie Schuster

CAIAPHAS

Andreas Richter   Maximilian Stöger

ANNAS

Peter Stückl   Walter Fischer

JOSEPH OF ARIMATHEA

Walter Rutz   Christian Bierling

NICODEMUS

Jonas Konsek   Abdullah Kenan Karaca

SIMON THE LEPER

Matthias Müller   Hubert Schmid

PILATE

Anton Preisinger   Carsten Lück

LONGINUS, CENTURION

Markus Köpf

Ferdinand Meiler

HEROD

Simon Marschalek

Benedikt Fischer

NATHANAEL

Kilian Clauß

Sebastian Dörfler

ARCHELAUS

Simon Fischer

Tobias Eich

EZEKIEL

Julius Iven

Dima Schneider

JEHOSHAPHAT

Florian Maderspacher

Thomas Müller

ANGEL

David Bender

Michael Hollatz

VERONICA

Ursula Mayr

MUSICAL DIRECTION

Markus Zwink

Eva Kammerer

Dr. Christian Wolf

Oberammergau's Passion Play is inextricably linked to its music. As early as the 18th century, there are recurring references to a "choir" in the texts for the play, largely in connection with the explanatory text for the tableaux vivants. Scenes featuring allegorical figures and all manner of spirits from Hell which were established by 1800 were also performed by a "choir", but the records offer no named composer, and no scores have been handed down. It is only with the compositions of the Oberammergau teacher Rochus Dedler (1779–1822) that we get an idea of the music that accompanied Passion performances, and its scope. Contemporary reports indicate that there were eight singers on the scaffolding stage in the cemetery; in their function as "guardian spirits" or "geniuses" they accompanied more than 25 tableaux vivants with their singing. They were backed by a small orchestra of instrumentalists from Oberammergau and the surrounding area: a handful of strings along with a flute, two clarinets, horns, trumpets and timpani. So it was a particularly sparse setting of the Passion music presented to audiences at the time, which were already around 4,000 strong.

In the current Passion Play season there is a total of 125 choristers, and around the same number of instrumentalists making up the orchestra. At each of the 110 performances there are 57 musicians in the orchestra pit, and 64 singers in the choir, including the soloists. To make all this possible, the municipality of Oberammergau undertakes a wide range of musical development work. Talented singers and instrumentalists receive individual support, and there is a wide variety of instrumental groups and choirs for every age group. Here children and young people can try their hand and build on their skills until they finally get to experience the Passion Play as a member of the orchestra or choir.

ORCHESTRA

SOLOISTS

SOPRANO

Dominika Breidenbach

Maria Buchwieser

Katharina Osterhammer

Franziska Zwink

Maria Zwink

CONTRALTO

Caroline Fischer-Zwink

Monika Gallist

Veronika Pfaffenzeller

Antonie Schauer

Gabriele Weinfurter-Zwink

TENOR

Michael Etzel

Korbinian Heinzeller

Moritz Kugler

Michael Pfaffenzeller

BASS

Heino Buchwieser

Anton Sonntag

Josef Zwink

CHOIR

Acknowledgements

We, the management team of the Passion Play 2022, would like to thank all employees without whose work this book would never have appeared: our assistants Kilian Clauß (assistant to the director), Elena Scheicher and Lorenz Stöger (assistant to the set and costume designer). The following names stand for the production workshops responsible for the stage sets: our technical manager Carsten Lück and the workshop employees, Florian Bartl (workshop manager), Tobias Haseidl (head sculptor), Christian Huber (stage painter) and Sarah Hesse (props). Our special thanks go to Susanne Eski (head of wardrobe), Anna Schories (production manager), Christiane Gassler and Rosi Pongratz, as well as to Kathrin Zintl and Lena Bader (make-up) for their work in developing over 2,000 costumes. Many thanks also to Valentin Rott, Ferdinand Dörfler, Sebastian Schulte, Benjamin Mayr, Viktoria Bischl and Thilo Feldmeier.

Credits

This book marks the 42nd Oberammergau Passion Play
from 14 May to 2 October, 2022
Director: Christian Stückl
Set and costume designer: Stefan Hageneier
Musical director and composer: Markus Zwink
Conductors: Eva Kammerer, Dr. Christian Wolf
Second director: Abdullah Kenan Karaca
Lighting: Günther E. Weiß, Martin Feichtner

Illustrated book

Photography: Birgit Guðjónsdóttir
Lighting design: Niels Maier, Matthias Feldmeier
Photo assistant: Johannes Neumann
Lithography: Marc Teipel
Image editing: Holger Herschel
Design: Kerstin Bigalke
Translation: James J. Conway
Editorial: Nicole Gronemeyer
Production: Paul Tischler
Printing and binding: aprinta druck GmbH

Photo credits

All pictures in this book are by Birgit Guðjónsdóttir, except for
Arno Declair: p. 148 (b.l.)
Gabriela Neeb: p. 170–172, 174 (14 pictures)
Sebastian Schulte: p. 140–142, 143 (t., b.r.), 144, 145 (t.l., b.), 146 (t.),
147 (b.), 148 (t., b.m., b.r.), 149 (b.), 151 (b.r.), 152 (t., b.m., b.r.), 153 (b.),
167 (b.r.), 174 (2 pictures)
Andreas Stückl p. 143 (b.l.), 145 (t.), 146 (b.), 149 (t.), 150 (b.l., b.m.),
151 (b.l.), 152 (b.l.), 153 (t.), 168 f., 174 (1 picture)

The historic images in the Chronicle are from the Municipal
Archive Oberammergau.

Bible quotations are taken from the King James Bible.

Printed in Germany

ISBN 978-3-95749-284-5 (trade edition)
ISBN 978-3-95749-439-9 (edition of the Passion Play Oberammergau)

PEFC Certified
This product is from sustainably managed forests and controlled sources
PEFC/04-32-0928   www.pefc.co.uk

Published by the Municipality of Oberammergau

Reproduction of the official illustrated book "Passion Play Oberammergau 2022" or parts thereof in any form or use of it for any media, publications, events of any kind is forbidden without the express permission of the Municipality of Oberammergau.

2022
PASSION
PLAY
OBERAMMERGAU

Theater der Zeit

Publisher: Harald Müller
Winsstraße 72, 10405 Berlin, Germany
www.theaterderzeit.de

Obe=